EVEN MORE TRUE STORIES

An Intermediate Reader

Longman

by Sandra Heyer

INTRODUCTION

Even More True Stories is an intermediate reader for students of English. It consists of 15 units centered around high-interest stories adapted from newspapers and magazines. The vocabulary and structures used in the stories are carefully controlled to match those of a typical intermediate ESL course. At the same time, all attempts have been made to keep the language natural.

PRE-READING

A photograph introduces each unit. Pre-reading activities motivate students to read, encourage predictions about the content of the reading, and prompt students to share knowledge and experiences about the topic.

READING THE STORY

Some students might find it helpful to first skim the story by reading the first paragraph and the first sentences of subsequent paragraphs. Students who stop at each unfamiliar word should be encouraged to read silently twice, once without stopping, and then again, stopping to circle new vocabulary.

When all the students have finished reading, the teacher clarifies new vocabulary. If the students read at home, they use the vocabulary exercises to help clarify new words. The teacher may read the selection aloud while the students follow along in their texts.

Teachers might also point out organizational devices used in the stories, such as introductory anecdotes, topic sentences, transitions, and conclusions.

THE EXERCISES

Each unit offers a variety of post-reading exercises. Both the choice and the use of the exercises are flexible and will depend on the individual teaching environment and style. Students can work individually, in pairs, or in small groups. The answer key at the back of the book affords the teacher a choice in the method of correcting the exercises.

Vocabulary. The vocabulary exercises are designed to aid comprehension by helping define unfamiliar words. The unfamiliar words in each story were identified by students who participated in field-testing the stories. The words that most students designated as "new" and that could be clearly explained were included in the exercises.

Looking at the Story encourages guessing meaning through contextual clues.

Looking at a New Context is the supplemental vocabulary exercise in some units. Students demonstrate that they understand the meaning of the new words by using them in contexts that are relevant to their own lives. They complete sentences such as "Someone I admire is _____." In class, students read their completed statements aloud in small groups. Students are encouraged to respond to one another's statements with questions and comments such as "Why?" or "Really?" These comments often prompt discussions based on the new vocabulary.

Looking at Special Expressions is the supplemental vocabulary exercise in other units. Because idiomatic expressions are best clarified through a combination of definition and example, the definition of each expression is followed by a matching exercise that offers three examples of the expression in use.

Comprehension. The comprehension exercises are not intended to test the students' understanding of the reading as much as to introduce reading skills that will foster comprehension.

Understanding the Main Ideas is a multiple-choice exercise. Students either circle the correct information or draw a line through the information that is not in the story. The latter task is a subtle introduction to outlining: what remains after the incorrect information is crossed out is an outline of the story.

Understanding Supporting Details is a matching exercise. As students match main ideas with "examples," they learn to identify supporting details.

Understanding Details recycles some of the vocabulary from the vocabulary exercises, verifies comprehension, and encourages the development of scanning techniques.

Scanning for Information helps students learn to scan quickly for names, dates, place names, and numbers.

Understanding Cause and Effect focuses the students' attention on relationships expressed by the word *because*.

Understanding Time Relationships helps students establish the sequence in which information or events are reported.

Discussion and Writing. Two spin-off exercises end each unit. A discussion exercise asks students to personalize the ideas and themes presented in the reading by discussing questions with classmates, sharing opinions, and exchanging information about their respective countries. Many of the discussion exercises require students to complete an activity in pairs or small groups so that all students—even those in large classes—have a chance to participate.

The final exercise is a guided writing based on the reading. The examples are the work of intermediate-level ESL students.

Challenge Pages. The Challenge pages are a new feature in this second edition of *Even More True Stories*. They are intended to do what the rubric suggests: provide a challenging reading experience for students who are ready for more difficult material. The level of difficulty in the Challenge pages is a half-step up from the main story. The Challenge pages were written for an audience whose native language is English, with no special consideration given to vocabulary or sentence structure. The intent of the Challenge pages is to facilitate the transition from controlled to authentic written English. Students who participated in field-testing the Challenge pages seemed to take pride in knowing they were reading "real English," not English written specifically for the ESL student.

The stories, the exercises, and the Challenge pages are intended to build students' confidence along with their reading skills. Above all, it is hoped that reading *Even More True Stories* will be a pleasure, for both you and your students.

CONTENTS

Unit **1** Brats 2

Unit **2** More Alike Than Different 10

Unit **3** The World's Largest Family 18

Unit **4** Healthy Again 26

Unit **5** The Buried City 34

Unit **6** Misunderstandings 42

Unit **7** A Real Bargain 50

Unit **8** Black Cats and Broken Mirrors 58

Unit **9** A Killer in the Backseat 66

Unit **10** The Treasure Hunt 74

Unit **11** The Plain People 82

Unit **12** Postponing Death 90

Unit **13** An Unexpected Adventure 98

Unit **14** Sucker Day 106

Unit **15** Love Under Siege 114

Answer Key 122

UNIT 1

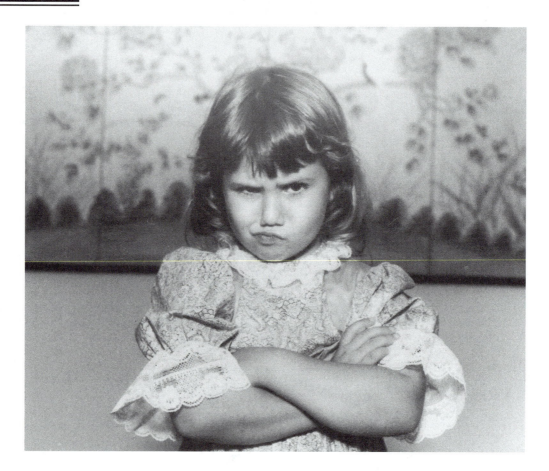

1. PRE-READING

Look at the picture and think about these questions. Discuss your answers with your classmates.

- The girl in the picture is named Lizzie. What kind of a girl do you think Lizzie is? Do you think she does what her parents want her to do? Do you think she usually behaves or misbehaves?
- If you guessed that Lizzie often misbehaves, you were right. She threw her mother's wedding ring into the toilet and put ice cream into the VCR. She is a brat. (*Brat* is not a polite word.)
- In this story, you will read about Lizzie and other brats. Have you ever known any brats? What did they do when they misbehaved?

Brats

A few years ago a French toy company had an unusual contest—a "biggest brat" contest. The company had a prize for the child whose behavior was the worst in the world. Over 2,000 parents entered their children in the contest. "Our child is the world's biggest brat!" they wrote. The parents made lists of all the bad things their children had done. Judges read the lists and chose the winner. She was a little girl from the United States. Her name was Lizzie, and she was four years old. Here are a few of the things Lizzie did to win the title "The World's Biggest Brat":

- She put a garden hose into the gas tank of her father's car. Then she turned on the water.
- She painted a leather sofa with spray paint.
- She threw her mother's wedding ring into the toilet. Then she flushed the toilet.
- She put an ice-cream sandwich into the VCR.
- She set the table for dinner. Then she glued the silverware to the table. Imagine her parents' surprise when they sat down to eat and tried to pick up their forks!

Lizzie may be the world's biggest brat, but she is certainly not the world's only brat. Alo is a five-year-old boy from Bangladesh. One afternoon, while his father was asleep on the sofa, Alo cut off his father's mustache. A few days later, he cut off his brother's eyebrows when his brother was sleeping in the bedroom. A few weeks after that, he cut off most of his mother's hair when she was asleep at night. Alo's family now keeps every pair of scissors under lock and key and always sleeps behind locked doors.

The behavior of a Mexican boy named Manuel is perhaps even worse than Lizzie's and Alo's because it is more dangerous. Manuel likes to play with matches. One day he found some matches near the kitchen stove. He took the matches, sneaked into his parents' bedroom, and set fire to the curtains. Fortunately, Manuel's mother walked into the bedroom just in time. She pulled down the curtains and put out the fire before it spread.

Hiroshi, a young Japanese man, says that he rarely misbehaved when he was a young child but turned into a real brat when he was about thirteen. "My friends and I used to sneak around at night and let the air out of tires. We were terrible," he says. "Our parents tried to control us, but they didn't have much success. We drove them crazy."

No mother or father wants to be the parent of a brat. Parents everywhere try to control their children's behavior. Some parents spank their children when they misbehave. Other parents won't let their children watch TV or eat dessert. In Japan, parents often send their children outside when they misbehave and tell them they can't come into the house. In the United States, parents do just the opposite: They send their children to their bedrooms and tell them they can't go outside.

Lizzie's parents don't know what to do about Lizzie. Her mother says, "I keep telling myself that Lizzie is going through a stage, but sometimes I don't know. . . . It seems like she's always getting into trouble." Lizzie's father says, "One day we'll look back on all this and laugh."

What does Lizzie think about her behavior? Lizzie doesn't like to talk about it. When a reporter asked Lizzie if she was "a bad girl," Lizzie kicked his leg. Then she yelled, "I'm not a brat! I'm an angel! Get out of my house!"

2. VOCABULARY

LOOKING AT THE STORY

Write the correct word on the line.

hose	sneaked	kicked	glued	scissors	leather
prize	curtains	silverware	misbehaves	rarely	fortunately

1. The French toy company gave Lizzie's family a _____. They got money and some toys because Lizzie was the winner of the contest.

2. Lizzie doesn't do what her parents tell her to do. She _____.

3. The sofa that Lizzie painted was very expensive; it was made of _____.

4. People usually use a _____ to water their gardens, but Lizzie used it to put water in the gas tank of her father's car.

5. When Lizzie's family sat down to eat, they couldn't pick up their knives, forks, and spoons because Lizzie had _____ the _____ to the table.

6. Alo used a pair of _____ to cut his family's hair while they were sleeping.

7. When no one was looking, Manuel took some matches. Then, walking quietly, he _____ into his parents' bedroom.

8. In the bedroom Manuel set fire to the _____ on the window.

9. Manuel's mother was lucky. When Manuel set fire to the curtains, she walked into the bedroom at that moment and put out the fire before it spread. _____, she walked into the room just in time.

10. Did Hiroshi misbehave as a young child? "Not often," he says. "When I was young, I _____ misbehaved."

11. When a reporter asked Lizzie if she was a "bad girl," Lizzie hit him with her foot. She _____ the reporter.

LOOKING AT A NEW CONTEXT

Complete the sentences to show that you understand the meanings of the new words. In small groups, take turns reading your sentences aloud. Ask your classmates questions about their sentences.

1. A child I know who often misbehaves is _____.

2. Something I rarely do is _____.

3. I feel fortunate because _____.

4. I would like to give my _____ a prize for _____.

3. COMPREHENSION/READING SKILLS

UNDERSTANDING THE MAIN IDEAS

What information is not in the story? Draw a line through the information.

1. The winner of the "biggest brat" contest
    a. was named Lizzie.
    b. was four years old.
    c. was from the United States.
    d. ~~had blond hair.~~

2. Lizzie
    a. filled the gas tank of her father's car with water.
    b. drew pictures on the living room wall.
    c. painted a leather sofa with spray paint.
    d. flushed her mother's wedding ring down the toilet.

3. Some other brats are
    a. Alo, who cut off his family's hair.
    b. Marie, who hits other children.
    c. Manuel, who plays with matches.
    d. Hiroshi, who used to let air out of tires.

4. Parents try to control their children's behavior by
    a. making them stand in a corner.
    b. spanking them.
    c. not letting them watch TV or eat dessert.
    d. sending them outside or to their bedrooms.

UNDERSTANDING DETAILS

Read the following sentences. One word in each sentence is not correct. Find the word and cross it out. Write the correct word.

1. A few years ago a ~~Korean~~ *French* toy company had an unusual contest.

2. The company wanted to find the child whose behavior was the best in the world.

3. Over 200 parents entered their children in the contest.

4. The parents made lists of all the good things their children had done.

5. The winner of the contest was a little boy from the United States.

Now copy three sentences from the story, but change one word in each sentence so that the information is not correct. Give your sentences to a classmate. Your classmate will find the incorrect word in each sentence, cross it out, and write the correct word. When your classmate is finished, check the corrections.

6. _____

_____

7. _____

_____

8. _____

_____

4. DISCUSSION

A. **Think about these questions. Discuss your answers with your classmates.**

1. When you were a child, were you a "brat" sometimes or were you always an "angel"? Can you remember anything bad you did? Tell your classmates about it.
2. What do you think about spanking children who misbehave?
3. Do you know a child who often misbehaves? What bad things does the child do?
4. Do you think children in different countries behave differently? Or do you think children everywhere behave the same way?

B. **Imagine that you are a parent in the following situations. In small groups, read about each problem and decide what you would do. Circle the answers your group chooses, or write your own answers.**

1. When you return home from shopping with your son, you discover a small toy in his pocket. He has stolen the toy from a department store. You

   a. spank him and send him to his room.

   b. let him keep the toy this time.

   c. go back to the store with him and return the toy.

   d. _____

2. You tell your teenage daughter to be home by 10:00 P.M. She wants to stay out later. As she leaves the house, she yells, "I hate living here!" and slams the door. You

   a. run after her to tell her that she has to stay home.

   b. run after her to tell her she must come back and leave the house again quietly.

   c. do nothing.

   d. _____

3. You are at a department store with your three-year-old daughter. She wants you to buy her a toy; you say, "No." She lies down on the floor and screams. You

   a. pick her up and carry her out of the store.

   b. buy her the toy.

   c. explain to her why she can't have the toy.

   d. _____

4. Your six-year-old son comes home crying. An older boy in the neighborhood has hit him. You

   a. tell the older boy never to hit your son again.

   b. talk to the older boy's parents.

   c. give your son karate lessons.

   d. _____

5. WRITING

Answer one of the questions from Discussion Exercise 4A in writing. Here is what one student wrote.

I remember something bad I did when I was in school. Our school was made of adobe—that's dried mud—and the walls were soft. My seat was next to a wall. One day I was bored and I pushed my pencil into the wall. It made a small hole. The next day I pushed my pencil into the hole again and made the hole deeper. Everyday I pushed my pencil deeper and deeper into the hole. Finally, my pencil went through the wall. Then I began making another hole. I was busy making holes in the wall for days. Then the teacher noticed the holes. She was very angry and moved my seat away from the wall. That was the end of hole-making, and I was bored again.

Challenge

PART 1

Psychiatrists at a university wondered if parents in some places had more trouble with their children than parents in other places. To find out, they asked parents in twelve different places to fill out a questionnaire about their children's behavior. The questionnaire asked parents, for example, if their children lied, stole, got in fights, or set fires. Then the psychiatrists tabulated the results of the 14,000 questionnaires. The questionnaires revealed that some parents did seem to have more problems with their children.

Look at the graph below. Then discuss these questions:

- In which places did parents report the most problems with their children?
- Where did parents report the fewest problems with their children?
- Is your country on the graph? If so, is it where you expected it to be? If not, where do you think it would be?
- The questionnaires were not completed in the same way in each place. In Puerto Rico, for example, interviewers read the questions to parents all over the island and wrote down the parents' answers. In Sweden, parents in an affluent suburb of Stockholm filled out the questionnaires at home and returned them to their children's schools. (84% of the questionnaires were returned.) In what ways could this difference have affected the results of the psychiatrists' study? (The answer is in the Answer Key.)
- If parents in some places really do have more problems with their children than other parents, what are some possible explanations?

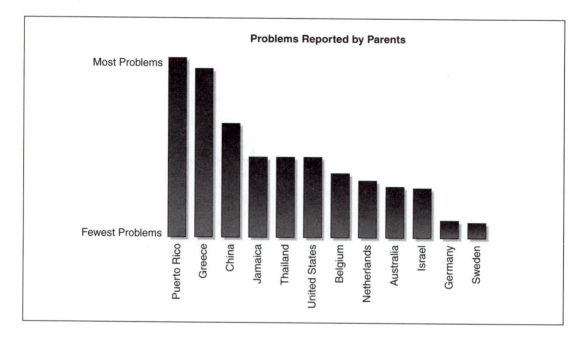

Problems Reported by Parents

Most Problems

Fewest Problems

Puerto Rico / Greece / China / Jamaica / Thailand / United States / Belgium / Netherlands / Australia / Israel / Germany / Sweden

PART 2

This questionnaire is similar to the one that parents in the twelve different places filled out. Read the questionnaire, and then think back to your own childhood. Complete the questionnaire as you think your parents would have completed it.

Circle 0 if the statement is not true of your child. Circle 1 if the statement is sometimes true of your child. Circle 2 if the statement is very true or often true of your child.

0	1	2	1. Argues a lot
0	1	2	2. Brags
0	1	2	3. Can't pay attention for long
0	1	2	4. Cries a lot
0	1	2	5. Is cruel to animals or other children
0	1	2	6. Destroys things
0	1	2	7. Is disobedient
0	1	2	8. Gets in fights
0	1	2	9. Has friends who get in trouble
0	1	2	10. Lies or cheats
0	1	2	11. Is a picky eater (eats only some things)
0	1	2	12. Refuses to talk
0	1	2	13. Runs away from home
0	1	2	14. Screams
0	1	2	15. Sets fires
0	1	2	16. Is stubborn
0	1	2	17. Swears
0	1	2	18. Has temper tantrums
0	1	2	19. Is very loud
0	1	2	20. Whines

Add the numbers you circled. That is your total score. If your total score is:

0–10	You were an angel!
11–20	You gave your parents a little trouble, but overall you behaved pretty well.
21–30	You gave your parents quite a bit of trouble—more than the average child.
31–40	You gave your parents a lot of trouble! They could have entered you in the "World's Biggest Brat" contest!

(Note: This questionnaire is just for fun. The actual questionnaire that psychiatrists gave parents was much longer and was scored differently.)

UNIT 2

1. PRE-READING

Compare gestures in your native country with gestures in other countries. Your teacher
will ask you the questions below. Answer the questions using only your hands. Do not
speak! As you answer each question, look at your classmates. Which gestures are the
same? Which gestures are different?

In your native country how do you say . . . ?

1. Come here.
2. Go away.
3. Stop.
4. Please be quiet.
5. I can't hear you.
6. You have a phone call.

7. Who, me?
8. Yes.
9. No.
10. I don't know.
11. Wait a minute.
12. He/She's crazy.

13. He/She's intelligent.
14. Money
15. A long time ago.
16. This is good.
17. This is bad.
18. This is delicious.

More Alike Than Different

Everyone listened attentively as the woman spoke.

"If you want to say 'OK,' don't make a circle with your thumb and first finger," the woman began. "That means OK here in the United States, but in Russia it's an obscene gesture."

The audience of 300 Americans chuckled; a few people took notes.

"It's all right to admire something," the woman continued, "but don't be too enthusiastic. Don't say, 'I *really* like your tablecloth.' Your Russian friend will offer you the tablecloth and will be offended if you don't take it."

"Remember that, in general, life in Russia is not as comfortable as life in the United States. You might not have hot running water, or you might have to share a bathroom with five or six people."

The woman was preparing the Americans for their trip to Russia. In Russia, the language, customs, and food would be different. Even simple things, like making a phone call, would be different. The Americans wanted to learn about these differences before their trip. They didn't want to experience culture shock.

When they arrived in Russia, the Americans were glad that they had prepared for their trip. Most of them experienced only a little culture shock. They enjoyed their visit and made a lot of Russian friends.

Making friends was, in fact, the purpose of the trip. The trip was planned by The Friendship Force, an international organization that promotes world peace. The Friendship Force believes that people who are friends will not fight wars. So, to help people from all over the world become friends, it organizes exchanges of people. The U.S.-Russian exchange was one of the largest exchanges it has ever organized. The Friendship Force sent 300 Americans to Russia and 300 Russians to the United States.

The Russians, like the Americans, prepared for their visit by learning about life in the other country. Still, they, too, experienced a little culture shock.

The Russians knew that Americans were fond of pets, but they were shocked to see pets inside homes. They couldn't believe their eyes when they saw dogs eating in the kitchen and sleeping on people's beds.

They were surprised at the difference between everyday life in Russia and in the United States. The Americans' lives, they said, were much easier. A Russian woman gasped when she saw an American pour rice directly from a box into a pan of boiling water. "You didn't wash the rice?" she asked. She explained that at home she had to wash the rice carefully and pick out all the stones. "Are you kidding?" the American said. "If people here had to do that, nobody would buy rice."

The Russians knew that Americans liked to eat fast food in restaurants, but they were disappointed to see that Americans ate fast meals at home, too. In Russia, the evening meal often lasts an hour or two because families sit at the table and talk. When American families eat together—*if* they eat together—they often eat quickly and don't take time for long conversations. The Russians thought that was a shame.

In spite of their differences in language and culture, the Russians and Americans became friends. The two women in the picture became friends, even though the Russian woman couldn't speak a word of English and the American woman couldn't speak a word of Russian. For two weeks they communicated through sign language and dictionaries.

Some of the Americans who traveled to Russia were schoolchildren from a sixth-grade class. When they returned to the United States, their teacher asked them to write about their trip. One 11-year-old girl wrote, "I have learned a lot from this experience. I learned to adapt to a different culture. And I learned that people all over the world are more alike than they are different."

2. VOCABULARY

LOOKING AT THE STORY

Read the following sentences. Then complete the statements. Circle the letter of the correct answer.

Everyone listened *attentively* as the woman spoke.

1. To listen attentively is to listen

    a. carefully.   **b.** nervously.

"Don't make a circle with your thumb and first finger," the woman said. "That's an *obscene* gesture in Russia." The *audience* of 300 Americans *chuckled*.

2. An obscene gesture is

    a. not polite.   **b.** polite.

3. An audience

    a. listens or watches.   **b.** sings, dances, or speaks.

4. To chuckle is to

    a. sing loudly.   **b.** laugh quietly.

"It's all right to *admire* something," the woman said, "but don't be too *enthusiastic*. Don't say, 'I *really* like your tablecloth.' Your Russian friend will offer you the tablecloth and will be *offended* if you don't take it."

5. If you admire something, you

    a. don't like it.   **b.** like it.

6. If you are enthusiastic, you are

    a. interested and excited.   **b.** bored and tired.

7. People who are offended are

    a. a little angry because their feelings are hurt.   **b.** a little nervous because they don't know what to do.

The Russians knew that Americans were *fond of* pets.

8. People who are fond of pets

    a. don't like pets.   **b.** like pets.

A Russian woman *gasped* when she saw an American pour rice directly from a box into a pan of boiling water. "You didn't wash the rice?" she asked.

9. People gasp when they are

    a. tired.   **b.** surprised.

The Russians knew that Americans liked to eat fast food in restaurants, but they were *disappointed* to see that Americans ate fast meals at home, too.

10. People who are disappointed are

    a. not happy.   **b.** happy.

An 11-year-old girl wrote, "I learned to *adapt* to a new culture. And I learned that people all over the world are more *alike* than they are different."

11. People who adapt

    a. don't change.   **b.** change.

12. "Alike" means

    a. the same.   **b.** strange.

LOOKING AT A NEW CONTEXT

Complete the sentences to show that you understand the meanings of the new words. In small groups, take turns reading your sentences aloud. Ask your classmates questions about their sentences.

1. Someone I really admire is _____.

2. Someone or something that makes me chuckle is _____.

3. People who immigrate to the United States probably find it difficult to adapt to

_____.

4. People who immigrate to the United States probably find it easy to adapt to

_____.

5. I would listen attentively if someone were talking about _____.

6. I would be disappointed if someone gave me _____ for my birthday.

7. I would be enthusiastic if someone invited me to _____.

8. I would gasp with surprise if I heard that _____.

3. COMPREHENSION/READING SKILLS

UNDERSTANDING THE MAIN IDEAS

Circle the letter of the best answer.

1. "More Alike Than Different" is about

    a. the language, customs, and food in Russia.

    b. the U.S.-Russian exchange of people that was organized by The Friendship Force.

    c. communicating through sign language and dictionaries.

2. The Friendship Force is

    a. an international organization that promotes world peace.

    b. an organization that prepares Americans for visiting Russia.

    c. an international organization of children who visit other countries.

3. The Friendship Force believes that

    a. people who live in Russia do not have comfortable lives.

    b. people who are friends will not fight wars.

    c. people who do not speak English will experience culture shock in the United States.

4. To help people become friends, The Friendship Force
   a. sends language teachers all over the world.

   b. mails letters all over the world.

   c. organizes exchanges of people.

5. The Americans prepared for their visit by
   a. experiencing culture shock.

   b. writing essays.

   c. learning about Russian life.

6. The Russians who visited the United States were shocked to see
   a. Americans eating rice.

   b. pets in people's homes.

   c. fast-food restaurants.

7. Although their languages and cultures were different, the Russians and the Americans
   a. ate the same food.

   b. became friends.

   c. had the same everyday lives.

UNDERSTANDING SUPPORTING DETAILS

Find the best way to complete each sentence. Write the letter of your answer on the line.

1. "It's all right to admire something, but don't be too enthusiastic. For example, _____

2. The Friendship Force organizes exchanges of people. For example, _____

3. The Russians were shocked to see pets inside homes. For example, _____

4. The Russians said that the Americans' lives were much easier than theirs. For example, _____

5. In spite of their differences in language and culture, the Russians and Americans became friends. For example, _____

a. they couldn't believe their eyes when they saw dogs eating in the kitchen.

b. the two women in the picture became friends, even though the Russian woman couldn't speak English and the American woman couldn't speak Russian.

c. don't say, 'I *really* like your tablecloth.'"

d. Russians have to wash their rice carefully, but Americans don't.

e. The Friendship Force sent 300 Americans to Russia and 300 Russians to the United States.

4. DISCUSSION

A. Are you and your classmates more alike than different? Find out. Sit in groups of three. Continue asking one another questions until you discover five things you have in common. (For example: "We all like cats. We all have birthdays in August.") Then report back to the class.

B. When people move to a new country, they often go through three stages. These are the stages of culture shock:

Stage 1: Arrival
- Everything is new and different
- Happy, excited

Stage 3: One to two years after arrival
- Can speak new language, understand customs, laugh at mistakes
- Adapted, feel "at home"

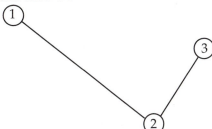

Stage 2: Six weeks to six months after arrival
- Everything in native country is better
- Sad, want to go home

Are you in a new country? If so, where are you—at stage 1, stage 2, stage 3, or somewhere in between? Put an X to show where you are. Then show a classmate where you put your X. Tell your classmate why you put your X where you did.

5. WRITING

Imagine that The Friendship Force is sending a group of people to your native country. What might surprise the visitors? Write about your native country. Prepare the visitors so that they don't experience culture shock. Here is what one student wrote.

Be careful when you shop in Syria. The prices you see in store windows are sometimes not the actual prices. For example, you might see a pair of shoes in a store window. Next to the shoes is the price. But when you go into the store, you find out that the real price of the shoes is more than the price in the window. So, Syrians don't always believe the prices they see in store windows. If people from other countries believe those prices, they will have a bad surprise.

Challenge

Test your knowledge of other cultures and customs. Imagine this: You are traveling around the world, and you find yourself in the situations described below.

Read about each situation. Then answer the question, circling the letter of the best answer. (The answers—and explanations of the answers—are in the Answer Key.)

1. You are visiting a temple in Thailand. In the courtyard of the temple, people are sitting on the ground. They are resting and talking. You are tired, so you sit down on the ground, too. You lean back on the temple wall and stretch your feet out in front of you. Thai people frown at you. You know you are doing something wrong. What is it?

   a. Only Thais sit on the ground at temples. People from other countries should stand or sit on a chair.

   b. Your back is against the wall of the temple. It is against the law to touch any part of a temple in Thailand.

   c. You are sitting with your feet stretched out in front of you. That means you are pointing your feet at people. It is very impolite.

2. You are in Korea. You get on a crowded city bus. There is no place to sit, so you stand. You are holding a big package. A woman who is sitting near you pulls at your package. What should you do?

   a. The woman is trying to tell you that it is illegal to get on a crowded bus with a big package. Get off the bus at the next stop and take a taxi.

   b. The woman wants to help you. Give her your package and smile.

   c. Thieves are common on crowded city buses. Hold on to your package tightly.

3. You are shopping in France. You are carrying a shopping bag full of things you bought at a department store. You walk into a small shop and look around. You don't see anything you want, so you leave. As you are leaving, you see that the shop owner is frowning at you. What have you done wrong?

   a. You carried your shopping bag around the small shop. You should have given it to the shop owner to hold for you.

   b. You were impolite. You didn't say "Bonjour" when you entered the shop, and you didn't say "Merci" when you left.

   c. You didn't buy anything. You should have bought something small, just to be polite.

4. You are at a tea shop in Nepal. The man next to you—a Nepali—pays five rupees for his cup of tea and leaves. When you get up to leave, the shop owner tells you the price of *your* cup of tea is seven rupees. What do you do?

   a. Be firm. Tell the shop owner you saw the other man pay only five rupees. Say that you'll pay only five rupees, too.

   b. Try to bargain the price down to at least six rupees.

   c. Ask again how much the tea is. If the shop owner says seven rupees again, pay the seven rupees.

5. You are studying at a university in the United States. In line at the cafeteria, you meet a friendly American student. You have a long conversation. You are new in the U.S. and

lonely. Here, you think, is a real friend. You exchange phone numbers, but your new friend doesn't call you. A week later, you see her again in the cafeteria. She smiles and says, "Hi," but she passes by your table to sit with some friends. What should you do?

a. Walk over to her table. Ask her, "Why didn't you call me?"

b. Forget her. She probably doesn't want to make new friends.

c. Call her once or twice. Invite her to do something together. If she always says she is busy, then forget her.

6. You have just moved to the United States. You want a telephone in your apartment as soon as possible. What should you do?

a. Go to a pay phone or to a friend's house. Call the telephone company. Take the first appointment that is available.

b. Go to the telephone company. Explain how important it is for you to get a phone as soon as possible.

c. Ask people if they know anyone who works at the telephone company. When you have the name of a telephone company employee, call the employee. Ask him/her to move your name to the top of the list.

7. You are living in Malaysia. You have a puppy. You have invited a Malaysian family, who is Muslim, to your house. What should you do about your puppy?

a. Put the puppy in another room, out of sight.

b. Invite your Malaysian guests to play with the puppy.

c. Be sure to tell your Malaysian guests that the puppy doesn't bite.

8. You are living in Italy. An Italian family invites you to visit them at 5:00 P.M. Two hours later, you and the family are still laughing and talking. They invite you to stay for dinner. You have no plans for dinner. You say,

a. "Yes, thank you," and stay.

b. "Yes, thank you, but only if I can help prepare dinner."

c. "Thank you, but I can't tonight. Let's get together for dinner another time."

9. You are living in Spain. You have to sign a paper in the presence of a notary public. So, you make an appointment with a notary public for 10:00 A.M. When you arrive at ten, a receptionist politely asks you to take a seat. At 11:30, you are still waiting for the notary. What should you do?

a. Tell the receptionist that you cannot wait any longer. Ask her to take you to the notary public's office immediately.

b. Walk past the receptionist and knock on the notary public's door.

c. Keep quiet and keep waiting.

10. At a party in France, you are introduced to a stranger. What is a good question to begin a conversation?

a. "Are you married?"

b. "What kind of work do you do?"

c. "Who did you vote for in the last election?"

UNIT 3

1.   PRE-READING

Look at the picture and think about these questions. Discuss your answers with your classmates.

- Do you come from a large family? Do your classmates come from large families? How many brothers and sisters do they have? Which classmate comes from the largest family?
- Your family or your classmate's family may be large, but it is not as large as the family of the man and woman in the picture. They have the world's largest family. They are the parents of 64 children.

The World's Largest Family

Mr. and Mrs. Albina don't know where all their grown children are living now. Some of them, they know, are in Argentina, but they aren't sure where in Argentina. They aren't sure how old all their children are, either. Ask them, for example, "How old is your daughter Susanna?" and they say, "We're not sure." They might even say, "Which Susanna?" But it is understandable that the Albinas can't keep track of their children's addresses and ages. After all, they have 64 children.

Mr. and Mrs. Albina, with 64 children, have the world's largest family. Not one of their children is adopted.

When people hear about the Albinas' large family, the first question they ask is, "How is it possible? How can one woman give birth to 64 children in her lifetime?" The answer is simple: Every time Mrs. Albina gave birth, she had twins or triplets. She was a triplet herself; she thinks that's why she always had twins or triplets.

The Albinas married when Mrs. Albina was 12 years old and Mr. Albina was 30. The children came quickly, in twos and threes. The first 21 children were boys. Mrs. Albina loved her sons, but she wanted a daughter very much.

The Albinas spent the early years of their marriage in Argentina. Then they decided to move to Chile. To travel from Argentina to Chile, they had to cross the Andes Mountains. Mr. and Mrs. Albina and their 21 sons made the difficult, two-week journey on mules. One night there was a terrible snowstorm in the mountains. During the snowstorm, Mrs. Albina gave birth to triplets, a boy and—two girls! Mrs. Albina now has 20 more girls, including twins who are 15 months old.

The oldest Albina children are in their thirties and forties. They are on their own now, but 18 of the Albina children still live with their parents. The family lives in a two-room shack in Colina, Chile. The shack has electricity but no toilet or running water. The children wash in a small bowl in the dusty backyard.

At times there is very little food in the Albinas' small house. When there is not enough food for everyone, Mrs. Albina makes sure the youngest children do not go hungry. "The smallest eat first, and then the bigger ones. We've always done it that way," she says. Obviously, the Albinas do not have enough money for their big family. Why, then, do they continue to have children?

The Albinas do not use birth control because it is against their religion. They could let other people take care of their children, but Mrs. Albina will not allow it. "When my two brothers and I were babies," she says, "our mother left us at an orphanage and never returned. We lived there together until we were five. Then a couple adopted my brothers, and I was left behind. I was heartbroken. I promised myself that when I became a mother, I would never give my children away. Even if I didn't have much money, I would always take care of my children myself." Mrs. Albina has kept her promise.

So, the Albina family continues to grow. Mr. and Mrs. Albina have so many children that they ran out of names for them all and had to give some children the same name. There are three Susannas, three Miriams, two Estrellas, and two Soledades.

Will there be a fourth Susanna or a third Estrella? Will the Albinas stop at 64 children, or will there be more? Mr. Albina is 79 years old, and Mrs. Albina is 61. "I'm getting old," she says with a smile. "I would like God to think of me and consider my age. But, if God sends more children to me, yes, there will be more."

2. VOCABULARY

LOOKING AT THE STORY

Write the correct word on the line.

shack	orphanage	consider	triplets	grown
obvious	adopted	mules	against	journey

1. Most of the Albina children are adults now, and they don't live with their parents. Where are they? Mr. and Mrs. Albina aren't sure. They don't know where all their _____ children are living.

2. Every time Mrs. Albina gives birth, she has two or three babies. She always gives birth to twins or _____.

3. When Mr. and Mrs. Albina moved from Argentina to Chile, they had to travel across the mountains. The _____ took two weeks.

4. Mr. and Mrs. Albina didn't have a car, and they had no money to take a bus. So, when they went to Chile, they rode on _____.

5. The Albinas' house has only two rooms, and it has no toilet or running water. It is a _____.

6. It is easy to see that the Albinas are poor. Their house is very small, and sometimes there is not enough food. It is _____ that they don't have enough money for their big family.

7. The Albinas' religion does not permit birth control. Birth control is _____ their religion.

8. Mrs. Albina's mother left her children at a home for children who have no parents, and she never returned to the _____ to get them.

9. When Mrs. Albina's brothers were five years old, a couple took them into their family. The boys were _____, but Mrs. Albina was left behind.

10. Will Mrs. Albina have more children? Yes, she says, if God sends them. But she is 61 years old. She hopes God will think about that. She hopes God will _____ her age.

LOOKING AT SPECIAL EXPRESSIONS

Find the best way to complete each sentence. Write the letter of your answer on the line.

to keep track of = to remember; to keep a record of

1. The Albinas can't ___c___

2. He uses a small notebook to _____

3. Could I use your telephone? I'll _____

a. keep track of my long-distance calls and pay you for them later.

b. keep track of his expenses.

c. keep track of their children's addresses and ages.

after all = it must be remembered

4. It is understandable that the Albinas aren't sure where all their children are. After all, _____

5. I'm not surprised they did well on the English test. After all, _____

6. I know she hasn't finished the work, but after all, _____

to run out of = to have no more

7. Mr. and Mrs. Albina have so many children that _____

8. I can't make the cake because _____

9. He couldn't finish the test because _____

d. they've studied English for over six years.

e. she's very busy.

f. they have 64 children.

g. he ran out of time.

h. they ran out of names for them all.

i. I've run out of flour.

3. COMPREHENSION/READING SKILLS

UNDERSTANDING THE MAIN IDEAS

Circle the letter of the best answer.

1. How many people are in the world's largest family?
   a. 66: a mother, a father, and their 64 adopted children
   b. 23: a mother, a father, and their 21 sons
   c. 66: a mother, a father, and their 64 children

2. All of the Albina children are
   a. living in Argentina.
   b. in their thirties and forties.
   c. twins or triplets.

3. The Albina family is
   a. rich.
   b. middle class.
   c. poor.

4. The Albinas do not use birth control because
   a. they want to have as many children as possible.
   b. they don't know about birth control.
   c. it is against their religion.

5. Mrs. Albina will not let other people take care of her children because
   a. she is afraid other people won't take good care of them.
   b. she promised that she would always take care of her children herself.
   c. she has a lot of money and can take care of them herself.

6. Will the Albinas have more children?
   a. Yes.
   b. No.
   c. Maybe.

SCANNING FOR INFORMATION

The underlined information is not correct. Find the correct information in the story and write it. Work quickly; try to complete this exercise in three minutes or less.

1. The Albinas married when Mrs. Albina was 12 years old and Mr. Albina was <u>29</u>. *30*

2. The first <u>24</u> children were boys.

3. The Albinas spent the early years of their marriage in <u>Peru</u>.

4. Then they decided to move to <u>Bolivia</u>.

5. The Albinas and their sons made the <u>three</u>-week journey across the Andes Mountains on mules.

6. During a snowstorm Mrs. Albina gave birth to <u>twins</u>.

7. Mrs. Albina now has <u>14</u> more girls.

8. The Albinas live in a two-room shack in <u>Santiago</u>, Chile.

9. Mrs. Albina and her brothers lived together at the orphanage until they were <u>four</u>.

10. There are <u>two</u> Miriams.

4. DISCUSSION

A. First, answer the questions yourself. Then ask a classmate the questions. Talk over the answers with your classmate.

	You	Your Classmate
1. How many brothers and sisters does your mother have?		
2. How many brothers and sisters does your father have?		
3. How many brothers and sisters do you have?		
4. If you are married: How many children do you have? If you are not married: Do you want to have children someday? How many?		
5. How many children are in the ideal family? (Is one child best? Two children? Five children?)		
6. How many children do most families in your country have today?		
7. Are families in your country getting bigger or smaller?		
8. Does your country have too many people?		
9. Does the government try to control population in your country?		

Now work as a class and answer the following questions.

1. Which classmate has the most aunts and uncles?
2. Which classmate has, or wants to have, the most children?
3. Do your classmates agree on the number of children in the ideal family?
4. In which countries are families getting bigger? Getting smaller? Staying the same size?
5. Which countries have too many people?

B. **Talk about your family with a partner. First, take a piece of paper. On the paper, draw a square for each person in your family. Do not draw inside the squares. Now imagine that your paper is a page from a photo album and that each square is a photo of someone in your family. Show your "album" to your partner. Tell your partner about each person in your family. Then listen while your partner describes the people in his or her family.**

5. WRITING

Write about your family or your partner's family. Here is what one student wrote.

I came from a traditional family in Taiwan. There are six people in my family: my parents, an older brother, and two older sisters. I'm the youngest.

My father started his own company 25 years ago. He's going to retire at the end of this Chinese year. I hope he'll be able to relax and enjoy life a little more then. My mother is a traditional Chinese housewife. I think she is one of the reasons my father has been successful. She has always taken care of our home so that my father could concentrate on his career. My two sisters are both in Japan now; one is married to a Japanese man, and the other studies at a music college in Tokyo. My brother is a swimming coach at a private health club. My brother and I are good friends.

My family, I guess, is ordinary but means a lot to me.

Challenge

Read the descriptions of these two families. Joanne Schmitt and Bill McKibben have very different ideas. Which ideas do you agree with? Why?

Full House

On a late summer afternoon, Bob Schmitt is barbecuing dinner for his family. About 30 hamburgers sizzle on the grill.

Inside the house, his wife, Joanne, is calmly sewing while her children buzz around her. Two daughters are setting the oversized table for dinner. Another daughter is making lemonade. One son is playing with a yo-yo, and another is playing Nintendo. A daughter is reading a magazine, and a son is watching TV. Another

daughter is looking for a lost library book. A set of nine-year-old twins are playing a board game, while another set of twins are arguing. It's just another normal day at what Joanne Schmitt calls "the zoo"—the home she and Bob share with their 16 children.

Joanne and Bob have eight times more children than the average U.S. family, yet Joanne thinks there is nothing unusual about her family. "We eat like everyone else, sleep like everyone else, do family things just like everyone else," she says. "We just do it in quantity."

"In quantity" aptly describes the everyday life of the Schmitts. When Joanne shops for groceries, she buys the largest size of everything. She goes grocery shopping every two weeks, a two-and-a-half hour, $500 ordeal. The Schmitts have an extra refrigerator and an extra freezer in the basement so they can buy large amounts of whatever is on sale.

The Schmitts have to be careful with money. Although Bob makes a good salary as a computer specialist, they are on a tight budget. The younger children rarely get new clothes; nearly all their clothes are hand-me-downs from older siblings. Joanne cuts all her children's hair. The family never eats out except for an occasional trip to McDonald's, and their family vacations are always camping trips.

The tight budget is one drawback of having such a large family; the effort it takes just to keep track of everyone is another. Joanne confesses that she has a special calendar for her children's birthdays so she can keep them all straight. And she says she can't always get her children's names quite right. When her son Benny tried to put his little sister on his shoulders, Joanne said, "Danny . . . I mean Teddy . . . I mean Benny, don't pick her up!" Once the Schmitts went to the zoo, and when they got there, they realized they'd left five-year-old Rebecca, who was taking a nap, at home. (When she awoke and found herself alone in the house, Rebecca walked over to a neighbor's.)

In spite of the work, in spite of the tight budget, and in spite of the occasional moments of chaos, Joanne says she has never regretted having so many children. "Sixteen children have multiplied my worries, but they have also multiplied my joys," she says.

Joanne is 47 years old, and she is not planning on having any more children, although she and Bob are doing nothing to prevent them from coming; birth control is against their religion. Joanne says, "It's my religious belief that we were meant to fill the earth. That's why God made man and woman. But I think God's done with me . . . I hope God's done with me now."

Maybe One

Bill McKibben and his wife have a four-year-old daughter, Sophie, whom McKibben calls "the light of my life." Although McKibben loves his daughter and loves being a father, he and his wife will never have any more children. They made the choice to have only one child.

Bill McKibben is an environmentalist who believes the earth is threatened by overpopulation. The problem, he says, is not lack of space. The entire world population could fit into Texas and each person could still have an area equal to the floor space of the typical U.S. house. The problem is consumption—that people are using so much more of the earth's resources than their ancestors did.

In hunter-gatherer days, each person used about 2,500 calories a day. People killed animals, picked berries, burned firewood, and built shelters. Each person needed only a small amount of the earth's resources to survive. Today we human beings seem to need more. We need energy to grow, store, and cook our food. We need energy to heat and cool our houses. We need energy to run our washing machines and cars, our hair dryers and our TVs. Each person in the world uses 31,000 calories a day, most of it in the form of fossil fuel; each person in the United States uses six times more than that.

McKibben believes this consumption is taking its toll on the environment, mainly by polluting the atmosphere with toxic gases like carbon dioxide. He says, "In the last thirty years, our impact has grown so much that we're changing even those places we don't inhabit; changing the way the weather works, changing the plants and animals that live at the poles and deep in the jungle . . . We've already done deep and systemic damage."

McKibben thinks that persuading people to consume less is hopeless. It would be easier, he thinks, to convince them to have only one child. That is what he tries to do in his book, *Maybe One.* He titled the book *Maybe One* because he wants to emphasize that couples should limit their family size not by force, but by choice.

McKibben anticipates that some people might argue that only children are spoiled and selfish. He maintains that is simply not true. The first research on only children was done in 1895 by G. Stanly Hall, a psychologist, who concluded that the only child had so many problems, "being an only child is a disease in itself." Hall's research was primitive by today's standards, but it created the myth of the troubled only child. More recent research shows that only children are, in fact, not much different from children with siblings, except that they tend to achieve more. McKibben reminds us that Leonardo da Vinci, Jean-Paul Sartre, Hans Christian Andersen, and Elvis Presley were all only children.

McKibben practices what he preaches. Shortly after his daughter was born, McKibben had a vasectomy. For McKibben and his wife, it is not "maybe one" child; it is definitely only one.

UNIT 4

1.   PRE-READING

Look at the picture and think about these questions. Discuss your answers with your classmates.

- The fish have needles in their backs. Have you ever seen needles like these? What are they used for?
- Why do you think the fish have needles in their backs?

Healthy Again

Mr. Cho was worried. Something was wrong with his goldfish. They had red patches on their skin, they weren't eating, and they didn't have much energy. Mr. Cho thought the fish probably had an infection. To cure the infection, he stuck needles into the backs of the fishes. That may seem unusual to some people, but it didn't seem unusual to Mr. Cho. Mr. Cho is an acupuncturist—a person who uses needles to treat illness and pain.

Mr. Cho left the needles in the fish for several minutes and then took them out. During the next few days he repeated the treatments. Soon the fish began to feel better. They swam with more energy and started to eat again, and the red patches on their skin disappeared. Did the fish get better because of the acupuncture treatments? Mr. Cho thinks so.

Although acupuncture for goldfish is uncommon, acupuncture for people is very common in Asia. Acupuncturists there help people who have medical problems like infections, backaches, and stomachaches. They even use acupuncture during operations so that patients don't feel pain.

To see what happens during an acupuncture treatment, let's imagine that Ming, a man who often has headaches, decides to go to Dr. Han, an acupuncturist. This is what might happen at Dr. Han's office.

First, Dr. Han examines Ming and asks him about his headaches. There are many kinds of headaches, and Dr. Han needs to know what kind of headaches Ming has.

Then Dr. Han decides where to insert the needles. Ming is surprised when Dr. Han tells him that she will insert needles in his neck and foot, but none in his head. That is not unusual. Often acupuncture needles are not inserted in the place where the patient feels pain.

Next, Dr. Han chooses the needles, which range in size from one-half inch long to six inches. Dr. Han chooses one-inch needles for Ming and begins to insert them. Ming feels a little pinch when each needle goes in. That is not unusual, either. Some patients say it hurts a little when the needles go in; other patients say it doesn't hurt at all. The needles stay in place for 15 minutes. Then Dr. Han removes them. Before he goes home, Ming makes an appointment to see Dr. Han in a week. Dr. Han says that Ming will know in a few weeks if the treatments are working.

Acupuncture has helped millions of people, not only in Asia, but all over the world. People say that acupuncture works. But *how* does it work?

One explanation of how acupuncture works is thousands of years old. The ancient Chinese, who were the first to use acupuncture, believed that energy flowed through the human body. They thought that sometimes too much energy—or too little energy—flowed to one part of the body. That caused pain or sickness. There were, however, several hundred places on the body where an acupuncturist could change the flow of energy. Those places were called acupuncture points. A needle inserted into an acupuncture point on a patient's leg, for example, changed the flow of energy to the patient's stomach. When the energy flowed correctly again, the patient would feel better.

There is also a modern explanation of how acupuncture works. Scientists point out that the acupuncture points have many more nerve endings than other places on the skin. Nerve endings receive pain messages when someone is sick or hurt. The pain messages then travel through the nerves. Perhaps acupuncture also sends messages through the nerves. These messages interrupt pain messages that are on their way to the brain. Because the pain messages never reach the brain, the patient feels better.

People who have been helped by acupuncture probably don't care which explanation is correct. They are just happy to be like Mr. Cho's fish—healthy again.

2. VOCABULARY

LOOKING AT THE STORY

Which words have the same meaning as the words in the story? Circle the letter of the correct answer.

1. The fish had red *patches* on their skin.
   - **a.** places that looked different from the area around them
   - **b.** places where acupuncturists insert needles

2. Mr. Cho wanted to *cure the infection.*
   - **a.** learn about the fish
   - **b.** make the sickness go away

3. He *stuck* needles into the backs of the fishes.
   - **a.** threw
   - **b.** pushed

4. An acupuncturist is a person who uses needles to *treat* illness and pain.
   - **a.** try to cure
   - **b.** cause

5. During the next few days he *repeated the treatments.*
   - **a.** watched his fish very carefully
   - **b.** stuck needles into the backs of the fishes again

6. Acupuncture for fish is *uncommon.*
   - **a.** difficult
   - **b.** unusual

7. Dr. Han decides where to *insert* the needles.
   - **a.** put in
   - **b.** buy

8. The needles *range in size* from one-half inch long to six inches.
   - **a.** The smallest needles are one-half inch, the largest are six inches, and there are other sizes in between.
   - **b.** The needles come in two sizes, one-half inch and six inches.

9. The ancient Chinese believed that energy *flowed* through the human body.
   - **a.** escaped
   - **b.** ran like a river

10. These messages *interrupt* pain messages that are on their way to the brain.
    - **a.** stop
    - **b.** help

LOOKING AT SPECIAL EXPRESSIONS

Find the best way to complete each sentence. Write the letter of your answer on the line.

to point out = to draw attention to; to say "Look at this" or "Think about this"

1. Scientists point out that acupuncture points _____
2. He pointed out that the bus we wanted to take _____
3. The students pointed out that the answers for Unit 9 _____

   a. arrived in Chicago in the middle of the night.
   b. were missing from the Answer Key.
   c. have many more nerve endings than other places on the skin.

3. COMPREHENSION/READING SKILLS

UNDERSTANDING THE MAIN IDEAS

What information is not in the story? Draw a line through the information.

1. What was wrong with Mr. Cho's goldfish?
   a. They had red patches on their skin.
   b. They weren't eating.
   c. ~~They had fevers.~~
   d. They didn't have much energy.

2. After the acupuncture treatments, Mr. Cho's fish
   a. swam with more energy.
   b. started to eat again.
   c. were sold for a lot of money.
   d. didn't have red patches on their skin anymore.

3. Acupuncturists in Asia use acupuncture
   a. to help people with backaches.
   b. to treat broken bones.
   c. to help people with stomachaches.
   d. during operations so that patients don't feel pain.

4. What happened before Dr. Han inserted the needles?
   a. She told Ming how much the treatment would cost.
   b. She examined Ming and asked him about his headaches.
   c. She decided where to insert the needles.
   d. She chose one-inch needles.

5. What happened during Ming's acupuncture treatment?
   a. Dr. Han inserted the needles.
   b. Ming felt a little pinch when each needle went in.
   c. Ming walked around the office.
   d. The needles stayed in place for 15 minutes.

6. What are some explanations of how acupuncture works?
   a. It corrects the energy flow in the body.
   b. It interrupts pain messages on their way to the brain.
   c. It changes the flow of blood through the body.

UNDERSTANDING SUPPORTING DETAILS

Find the best way to complete each sentence. Write the letter of your answer on the line.

1. Something was wrong with Mr. Cho's goldfish. For example, _____

2. The fish began to feel better. For example, _____

3. Acupuncture for people is very common in Asia. For example, _____

4. There were several hundred places on the body where an acupuncturist could change the flow of energy. For example, _____

a. acupuncturists there use acupuncture during operations so that patients don't feel pain.

b. a needle inserted into an acupuncture point on a patient's leg changed the flow of energy to the patient's stomach.

c. they swam with more energy and started to eat again.

d. they had red patches on their skin and they weren't eating.

4. DISCUSSION

A. Think about these questions. Discuss your answers with your classmates.

1. Do you think Mr. Cho's fish got better because of the acupuncture treatments?

2. Have you ever had a sick pet? What did you do? Some people take their sick pets to animal doctors. The pets get medicine and sometimes operations. What do you think about that?

3. Have you ever had an acupuncture treatment? If you have, tell your classmates about it. If you've never had an acupuncture treatment, would you try it?

B. Acupuncture is one type of medicine. There are many other types of medicine, too. Look at the seven types of medicine below. Each type of medicine has a treatment for headache. Read about the treatments. If you had headaches often, which types of medicine would you try? For each type of medicine, check (✔) "yes" or "no." Then ask a classmate, "Would you try it?" Ask about each type of medicine and check "yes" or "no." If your classmate answers "no," ask, "Why not?"

Type of Medicine	Common Treatment for Headache	Would You Try It?			
		YOU		YOUR CLASSMATE	
		Yes	No	Yes	No
1. Acupuncture	Insert one needle in the neck and another in the foot.				
2. Acupressure (also called Shiatsu)	With your fingertips, push on the back of the head and the sides of the forehead. Massage the hand between the thumb and the first finger.				
3. Chiropractic	Give a massage; move the bones in the spine so that the spine is straight.				

Type of Medicine	Common Treatment for Headache	Would You Try It?			
		YOU		YOUR CLASSMATE	
		Yes	No	Yes	No
4. Herbalism	Make tea by boiling a special plant or root. Give the tea to the patient, or give a pill made from the plant or root.				
5. Holistic Health Care	Treat not only the headache, but also mental or emotional problems that could be causing your headache.				
6. Spiritual Healing	Pray and put your hands on the person's forehead.				
7. Traditional Western Medicine	Give painkillers.				

Now work as a class and discuss these questions.

- Has anyone in the class tried these types of medicine?
- What was the medical problem?
- Did the treatment work?

5. WRITING

A. Imagine that you receive a letter from a friend. Your friend writes you that he has a medical problem and is going to try acupuncture. Your friend is afraid because he has never had an acupuncture treatment and doesn't know what will happen. Write a letter to your friend. Tell your friend what happens during an acupuncture treatment.

B. Have you ever needed medical treatment? What was the problem? Which type of medicine did you choose? What happened during the treatments? Did you get better? Write about your experience. Here is what one student wrote.

A few years ago I had a painful shoulder and decided to try acupuncture. Before I tried acupuncture, I was afraid of it. I thought, "That looks painful!" When I saw the long needles, I thought they would run through my body. But I was wrong. The needles were long, but the acupuncturist didn't insert the whole needle. He found the place where my shoulder hurt and inserted 30 needles. He inserted the needles little by little, and I didn't feel any pain. I went to the acupuncturist for about a month. After that, my shoulder was better.

Challenge

Acupuncture is relatively new in the United States and Great Britain. So people there sometimes exchange information about acupuncture on the Internet.

Below are three questions people asked an acupuncture news group on the Internet. Each question is followed by two answers. One answer is generally positive—that is, the person who wrote the answer had a good experience with acupuncture or knows someone who did. The other answer is generally negative—that is, the person who wrote the answer had a bad experience with acupuncture or knows someone who did.

Read each question and the two answers that follow it. Put a "P" next to the answer that is generally positive; put an "N" next to the answer that is generally negative.

Author: Joe Hyer <joehyer@hotmail.com>
Subject: Headaches

post reply ◀ prev next ▶

I just want to know if anyone has any suggestions because I am at the end of my rope! I have had the same headache for over a year now. I have been to countless neurologists, doctors, and chiropractors. I even went to a special headache clinic. Nothing has worked. Nothing showed up on the CT scan or MRI. Can acupuncture help? All I want to do is get rid of the pain, even if it's just for a day.

a. _____

Author: Sheri Beck <beck@ticon.net>
Subject: Re: Headache

post reply ◀ prev next ▶

I have a headache/acupuncture story--only it's not really mine, it happened to my mother-in-law. The acupuncturist told her to come in because she had a really bad headache. So she went in. The acupuncturist put some needles in and left. Then he came back and asked if she was feeling any better and she wasn't. He put more needles in and left. Well, he did this several more times--any better, no, more needles. In the meantime she was getting sicker (headache and stomachache). Finally, the last time he came back in, she said, "Oh, yes, it's much better" just to get those stupid needles out so she could go home and get her medicine. She said she never went back.

Sheri :-)

b. _____

Author: Teri Koop <koop@aol.com>
Subject: Re: Headache

post reply ◀ prev next ▶

I know acupucture doesn't work for everyone, but it was a miracle for me. It did what 5 years of medications could not. I'm pain-free for 6 months now--no headaches. It's great and I'd go back in a minute if I even felt the slightest pain again.

2

Author: Tony Horton <tony@hort.freeserve.co.uk>
Subject: Does acupuncture hurt?

post reply | prev | next

Tell me the truth . . . does acupuncture hurt? Even a little bit? How big are the needles?

a. _____

Author: Diana Parkinson <diana@brynford.freeserve.uk>
Subject: Re: Does acupuncture hurt?

post reply | prev | next

I can usually feel something, and sometimes something that I would go so far as to call pain. But it isn't at all severe, it's an almost nice tingly sort of pain.
The needles are a couple of inches long, but only about 1 cm goes into the skin.
Since starting acupuncture, I've come to learn there is a route back to the "joy of life" I had before.

b. _____

Author: David James <david_james@bigfoot.com>
Subject: Re: Does acupuncture hurt?

post reply | prev | next

It doesn't actually hurt, but I found it too stressful. When the needles went into my back, I felt my muscles like "paralyze." I was on my stomach, in this horrid trapped position for twenty-five mins. Afterward, I felt very relaxed, but during . . . argh! So I quit acupuncture.
Now I am interested in Chi Gong (sp?). There are no needles with Chi Gong.
You move your hands in directions to move energy through the body.

3

Author: Dan Comstock <dan@mailbag.com>
Subject: Acupuncture for Bad Knees?

post reply | prev | next

I'm a runner, and my knees are giving me trouble. Does anyone have experience with acupuncture for knee problems?

a. _____

Author: SPotter <potter@aol.com>
Subject: Re: Acupuncture for Bad Knees?

post reply | prev | next

My wife had a botched knee surgery which killed a lot of her nerve tissue in her left leg.

She was lying in bed screaming and crying for months. We used pain relievers with no help, so we went to an acupuncturist. The acupuncturist said it would cut the healing time in half, which it seemed to, according to an orthopedic surgeon. It was predicted that she would never walk normally again, and now she runs and backpacks.

b. _____

Author: afjones <afjones@infinet.com>
Subject: Re: Acupuncture for Bad Knees?

post reply | prev | next

My brother-in-law tried acupuncture for his bad knee (football injury), but he ended up having surgery anyway.
Many people will tell you of their wonderful experiences with acupuncture. They'll also tell you they saw Elvis Presley at the mall last weekend.

UNIT 5

1.   PRE-READING

Look at the picture and think about these questions. Discuss your answers with your classmates.

- What do you see in the picture? What do you think happened?
- The picture was taken at Pompeii. Where is Pompeii? Do you know what happened there? Tell your classmates what you know.

The Buried City

Every year thousands of tourists visit Pompeii, Italy. They see the sights that Pompeii is famous for—its stadiums and theaters, its shops and restaurants. The tourists do not, however, see Pompeii's people. They do not see them because Pompeii has no people. No one has lived in Pompeii for almost 2,000 years.

Once Pompeii was a busy city of 22,000 people. It lay at the foot of Mount Vesuvius, a grass-covered volcano. Mount Vesuvius had not erupted for centuries, so the people of Pompeii felt safe. But they were not safe.

In August of the year 79, Mount Vesuvius erupted. The entire top of the mountain exploded, and a huge black cloud rose into the air. Soon stones and hot ash began to fall on Pompeii. Then came a cloud of poisonous gas. When the eruption ended two days later, Pompeii was buried under 20 feet of stones and ash. Almost all of its people were dead.

Among the dead was a rich man named Diomedes. When the volcano erupted, Diomedes decided not to leave his home. The streets were filled with people who were running and screaming. Diomedes was probably afraid that he and his family would be crushed by the crowd. So, Diomedes, his family, and their servants—16 people all together—took some food and went down to the basement. For hours they waited in the dark, hoping the eruption would end. Then they began to cough. Poisonous gas from the mountain was filling the city. Diomedes realized that they had to leave. He took the key to the door, and a servant picked up a lantern. Together they walked upstairs. But the poisonous gas was already filling the house. When they were a few feet from the door, Diomedes and his servant fell to the floor and died. The 14 people downstairs died embracing one another.

For centuries Diomedes and his family lay buried under stones and ash. Then, in the year 1861, an Italian archeologist named Giuseppe Fiorelli began to uncover Pompeii. Slowly, carefully, Fiorelli and his men dug. The city they found looked almost the same as it had looked in the year 79. There were streets and fountains, houses and shops. There was a stadium with 20,000 seats. Perhaps most important of all, there were many everyday objects. These everyday objects tell us a great deal about the people who lived in Pompeii.

Many glasses and jars had a dark blue stain in the bottom, so we know that the people of Pompeii liked wine. They liked bread, too; metal bread pans were in every bakery. In one bakery oven there were 81 round, flat loaves of bread—a type of bread that is still sold in Italy today. Tiny boxes filled with a dark, shiny powder tell us that the women liked to wear eye makeup, and the jewelry tells us that pearls were popular in the year 79. Graffiti is everywhere in Pompeii. On one wall someone wrote "Romula loves Staphyclus." On another wall someone wrote "Everyone writes on these walls—except me."

Fiorelli's discoveries tell us much about the way the people lived. They also tell us much about the way they died.

One day Fiorelli was helping his men dig. When he tapped on the hard ash, he heard a hollow sound. He suspected that the space beneath was empty. As an experiment, he drilled a few holes in the ash and poured liquid plaster down the holes. When the plaster was hard, Fiorelli cleared away the ash. He found the plaster form of a man. The man's body had turned to dust long ago, but the ash had hardened around the space where the body had been.

During the next years Fiorelli filled dozens of spaces with plaster. The plaster forms show how the people of Pompeii looked in their last moments of life. Some have calm expressions on their faces; others look very afraid. Some people died holding their children. Others died holding gold coins or jewelry. Diomedes died with a silver key in his right hand, and his servant died holding a lantern.

Giuseppe Fiorelli, too, has died, but his work continues. One-fourth of Pompeii has not been uncovered yet. Archeologists are still digging, still making discoveries that draw the tourists to Pompeii.

2. VOCABULARY

LOOKING AT THE STORY

Which words or picture has the same meaning as the words in the story? Circle the letter of the correct answer.

1. Pompeii was *buried under* 20 feet of stones and ash.

   a. covered by   **b.** hit by

2. Diomedes, his family, and their *servants* went down to the basement.

   a. the people who worked in   **b.** the people who visited Pompeii
   their home

3. A servant picked up a *lantern.*

   a. light   **b.** knife

4. The 14 people downstairs died *embracing one another.*

   a. holding one another   **b.** arguing with one another

5. Slowly, carefully, Fiorelli and his men *dug.*

   a.   **b.**

6. There were streets and *fountains*, houses and shops.

   a.   **b.**

7. There was a *stadium* with 20,000 seats.

   a. large indoor theater   **b.** large sports field with rows
                                        of seats around it

8. There were also everyday *objects* that tell us a great deal about the people who lived in Pompeii.

   a. ideas   **b.** things

9. There were many glasses and jars with a dark blue *stain* in the bottom.

   a. juice made from purple grapes **b.** spot that can't be removed

10. *Graffiti* is everywhere in Pompeii.

    a. writing on the walls   **b.** garbage

11. When he *tapped on* the hard ash, he heard a hollow sound.

    a. hit lightly   **b.** listened to

12. He *suspected that* the space beneath was empty.

    a. told everyone that   **b.** thought that probably

LOOKING AT A NEW CONTEXT

Complete the sentences to show that you understand the meaning of the new words. In small groups, take turns reading your sentences aloud. Ask your classmates questions about their sentences.

1. A sight I would really like to see is _____.

2. My native city is famous for its _____.

3. If I had servants, I would ask them to _____.

4. Someone I often embrace is _____.

5. An everyday object I have that tells a great deal about me is _____.

6. If I were given permission to write graffiti on a city wall, I would write this:

_____.

7. Someone or something that always makes me feel calm is

_____.

3.   COMPREHENSION/READING SKILLS

UNDERSTANDING CAUSE AND EFFECT

Find the best way to complete each sentence. Write the letter of your answer on the line.

1. Tourists do not see Pompeii's people _____

2. The people of Pompeii felt safe _____

3. Diomedes decided not to leave his house _____

4. We know that the people of Pompeii liked bread _____

5. Fiorelli suspected that spaces beneath the ash were empty _____

a. because he was afraid that he and his family would be crushed by the crowd.

b. because he heard a hollow sound when he tapped on the ash.

c. because Pompeii has no people.

d. because Mount Vesuvius had not erupted for centuries.

e. because Fiorelli found metal bread pans in every bakery.

UNDERSTANDING TIME RELATIONSHIPS

"The Buried City" describes Pompeii at three different times: around the year 79, in the 1860s, and today. Read the sentences from the story. Decide what time the sentence tells about. Put a check (✔) in the right column.

	79	1860s	TODAY
1. Pompeii was a busy city of 22,000 people.	✔		
2. Tourists see the sights Pompeii is famous for, but they do not see its people.			
3. Mount Vesuvius erupted.			
4. Giuseppe Fiorelli began to uncover the city.			
5. Jewelry made of pearls was popular.			
6. Diomedes, his servants, and his family died.			
7. Fiorelli poured liquid plaster down the holes in the ash.			
8. Someone wrote "Romula loves Staphyclus" on a wall.			
9. Poisonous gas from the mountain filled the city.			
10. One-fourth of Pompeii is not yet uncovered.			

4. DISCUSSION

A. **Think about these questions. Discuss your answers with your classmates.**

1. Have you ever seen a volcanic eruption? Tell your classmates about it. Are there any volcanos in your native country? Where are they? Do they erupt sometimes?
2. The people of Pompeii lived at the foot of a volcano. That was a dangerous place to live. What cities today are in dangerous places? Why do people live there?
3. Do you know any other places that archeologists have uncovered or are still uncovering? Tell your classmates about them.

B. **When the volcano erupted at Pompeii, people who left took their most important possessions. Imagine that your home is on fire. Everyone who lives with you is safe, but your home will burn to the ground. There is time for you to save three of your possessions. Which possessions will you save?**

I will save

1. _____

2. _____

3. _____

Why are the possessions on your list important? Are they expensive? Were they gifts from special people? Are they things you can't buy? Show your list to a classmate. Explain why the things on your list are important to you.

5. WRITING

A. Write a description of one possession that is on the list you made in Discussion Exercise 4B. Explain why it is important to you. Here is what one student wrote.

If I could save one possession, I would save the letters from my friends. Before I came to the United States, one of my friends wrote me this letter:

"You will go to the United States soon. You may have many hard times before you adapt to your new environment. But don't forget that I am supporting you all the time. Even if I'm not close to you, I'll always be in your heart."

Every time I feel homesick, I read his letter. It always cheers me up. How could I ever replace a possession like that?

B. Every year thousands of tourists visit Pompeii. Have you ever been a tourist? Have you ever visited a beautiful or interesting place in your country or in another country? Write about it. Here is what one student wrote.

My Visit to Kyoto, Japan

I went to Kyoto in April this year. I stayed in a Japanese-style hotel. A mountain river ran past the hotel, and there was a wooden bridge over the river. From my hotel room I could see a mountain. The mountain was many colors of green, and at the foot of the mountain, there were many cherry blossoms. The green colors and the cherry blossoms were reflected on the river. It was a beautiful view. My heart softened.

Challenge

Read the paragraphs. They give you more information about the people and places of Pompeii. Then match each paragraph with the photo on the next page that fits it best. (Be sure to read the paragraphs to the end before you make your choice.) Write the number of the paragraph next to the photo.

1. It appears that when Vesuvius erupted, less wealthy people tried to leave the city, while wealthy Pompeiians stayed in their houses. The wealthy people were probably afraid that if they left, their houses would be looted when the eruption ended. So, they gathered up their most valuable possessions and ran to the strongest room in the house. When Fiorelli uncovered Pompeii, he sometimes found a whole family and their servants—all skeletons—together in one room of their house. The skeletons were surrounded by jewelry, coins, gold, and silver. In one house, a collection of beautiful silver was found hidden in the basement. All 115 pieces of silver were in perfect condition.

2. Houses in Pompeii did not have bathtubs because bathing was a recreational activity. Pompeii had four public baths, some for men and some for women. The layout of the baths indicates that bathers probably followed this routine: After checking their clothes, visitors took a cool bath to get clean. After the cool bath, they were massaged with fragrant oils. Then they were ready for the next four baths: a bath in warm water, a bath in very hot water (like the water in our Jacuzzis), another bath in warm water, and finally a bath in cool water. After their baths, the visitors could spend some time at the bath's library, swimming pool, or restaurant. Evidently, people stayed at the baths until well into the evening; 1,300 lamps were found at one bath.

3. Imagine driving your car to a city—let's say Paris— and discovering that you could not drive your car into Paris; you had to leave it parked outside the city. If you wanted to see Paris by car, you had to rent a Parisian car or travel by taxi. That was essentially the situation in Pompeii. Pompeii had a monopoly on transportation within its walls because of the way its streets were constructed. The stone streets of Pompeii filled with water during rainy weather. So that people could cross the streets without getting their feet wet, there were high blocks of stone at each intersection. The blocks of stone were always placed the same distance apart. Pompeiians knew what that distance was and built their chariots and carts so that the wheels passed on either side of the stepping stones. Few visitors to Pompeii had chariots that fit between the stepping stones, so most travelers had to leave their vehicles at the city gates. Cab drivers did a good business in Pompeii.

4. Visitors to Pompeii are amazed to see that some houses are identified by the owners' names. Signs in front of the houses say, for example, that this was the house of Diomedes or this was the house of Quintus Poppaeus. How did archeologists learn the names of some Pompeiians and figure out exactly where they lived? Actually, it was quite simple. Many Pompeiians were businessmen who kept their business records on wax tablets. Their names were on the tablets. So, if wax tablets labeled "Diomedes" were found in a house, it is almost certain that Diomedes and his family lived there. In some cases, we know not only the names of the people who lived in a house but what those people looked like. In the house of a man named Jucundus there was a bronze bust of a man— probably Jucundus himself. We know that Jucundus had big ears, thin hair, wrinkles on his forehead, and a large wart on his left cheek.

5. Pompeiians entertained themselves by watching gladiators fight. Pairs of gladiators, who were slaves or convicted criminals, generally fought until one man died. Gladiators who survived fight after brutal fight became heroes, much like our rock stars and great athletes. (When Pompeii was uncovered, the form of a woman wearing a lot of jewelry was found in the gladiators' barracks. Archeologists speculate that she had gone there to catch a glimpse of her favorite hero.) The contests of the gladiators were so popular that Pompeiians built a stadium just for the fights. With 20,000 seats, the stadium held almost the entire population of Pompeii.

a. _____

b. _____

c. _____

d. _____

e. _____

UNIT 6

1. PRE-READING

Below are pairs of English words that sound alike. Your teacher will say one word from each pair. Circle the word that you hear.

1. feel   fill
2. they   day
3. men   man
4. ice   eyes
5. cap   cup
6. glass   grass
7. hot   hat
8. thought   taught
9. thick   sick
10. jello   yellow
11. fifteen   fifty
12. bomb   bum
13. Oakland   Auckland

After you finish this exercise, your teacher will tell you the correct answers. Was the exercise difficult for you? If it was, don't worry—it's difficult for native speakers of English, too. In this story you will learn how the last two pairs of words caused *big* problems for people whose native language is English.

Misunderstandings

He had uncombed hair, dirty clothes, and only 35 cents in his pocket. In Baltimore, Maryland, he got on a bus and headed straight for the rest room. He thought that if he hid in the rest room, he could ride to New York without paying. But a passenger at the back of the bus saw him. She tapped the person in front of her on the shoulder and said, "There's a bum in the rest room. Tell the bus driver." That passenger tapped the person sitting in front of him. "Tell the bus driver there's a bum in the rest room," he said.

The message was passed from person to person until it reached the front of the bus. But somewhere along the way, the message changed. By the time it reached the bus driver, it was not "There's a *bum* in the rest room" but "There's a *bomb* in the rest room." The driver immediately pulled over to the side of the highway and radioed the police. When the police arrived, they told the passengers to get off the bus and stay far away. Then they closed the highway. That soon caused a 15-mile-long traffic jam. With the help of a dog, the police searched the bus for two hours. Of course, they found no bomb.

Two similar-sounding English words also caused trouble for a man who wanted to fly from Los Angeles to Oakland, California. His problems began at the airport in Los Angeles. He thought he heard his flight announced, so he walked to the gate, showed his ticket, and got on the plane. Twenty minutes after takeoff, the man began to worry. Oakland was north of Los Angeles, but the plane seemed to be heading west, and when he looked out his window all he could see was ocean. "Is this plane going to Oakland?" he asked the flight attendant. The flight attendant gasped. "No," she said. We're going to *Auckland*—Auckland, New Zealand."

Because so many English words sound similar, misunderstandings among English-speaking people are not uncommon. Not all misunderstandings result in highways being closed or passengers flying to the wrong continent. Most misunderstandings are much less serious. Every day, people speaking English ask one another questions like these: "Did you say seven*ty* or seven*teen*?" "Did you say that you *can* come or that you *can't*?" Similar-sounding words can be

especially confusing for people who speak English as a second language.

When a Korean woman who lives in the United States arrived at work one morning, her boss asked her, "Did you get a plate?" "No . . .," she answered, wondering what in the world he meant. She worked in an office. Why did the boss ask her about a plate? All day she wondered about her boss's strange question, but she was too embarrassed to ask him about it. At five o'clock, when she was getting ready to go home, her boss said, "Please be on time tomorrow. You were 15 minutes late this morning." "Sorry," she said. "My car wouldn't start, and. . . ." Suddenly she stopped talking and began to smile. Now she understood. Her boss hadn't asked her, "Did you get a plate?" He had asked her, "Did you get up late?"

English is not the only language with similar-sounding words. Other languages, too, have words that can cause misunderstandings, especially for foreigners.

An English-speaking woman who was traveling in Mexico saw a sign in front of a restaurant. The sign said that the special that day was *"sopa con jamón y cebollas."* She knew that was Spanish for "soup with ham and onions." That sounded good. As the woman walked to her table, she practiced ordering. She whispered to herself, *"Sopa con jamón y cebollas. Sopa con jamón y cebollas."* Then she sat down, and a waiter came to take her order. *"Sopa con jabón y caballos,"* she said. "What?" the waiter asked. No wonder the waiter didn't understand. The woman had just ordered a very unusual lunch: soup with soap and horses.

Auckland and *Oakland*. "A plate" and "up late." *Jamón* and *jabón*. When similar-sounding words cause a misunderstanding, probably the best thing to do is just laugh and learn from the mistake. Of course, sometimes it's hard to laugh. The man who traveled to Auckland instead of Oakland didn't feel like laughing. But even that misunderstanding turned out all right in the end. The airline paid for the man's hotel room and meals in New Zealand and for his flight back to California. "Oh well," the man later said, "I always wanted to see New Zealand."

2. VOCABULARY

LOOKING AT THE STORY

Which words have the same meaning as the words in the story? Circle the letter of the correct answer.

1. She *tapped the person* in front of her *on the shoulder.*

    a. touched the person's shoulder lightly with her hand   **b.** pushed hard on the person's shoulder

2. "There's a *bum* in the rest room."

    a. person who doesn't work and probably doesn't have a home   **b.** person who travels by bus

3. The driver *pulled over* to the side of the highway.

    a. looked   **b.** moved

4. The driver *radioed the police.*

    a. called the police on his radio   **b.** got the attention of a police car

5. That soon caused a *15-mile-long traffic jam.*

    a. line of stopped cars that was 15 miles long   **b.** line of cars going only 15 miles per hour

6. The police *searched the bus* for two hours.

    a. looked everywhere on the bus   **b.** drove everywhere with the bus

7. Twenty minutes after *takeoff,* the man began to worry.

    a. the plane went up into the air   **b.** the man took off his jacket

8. "Is this plane going to Oakland?" he asked the *flight attendant.*

    a. person who flies an airplane   **b.** person who takes care of the passengers on an airplane

9. Misunderstandings among English-speaking people are *not uncommon.*

    a. never happen   **b.** happen often

10. Not all misunderstandings *result in highways being closed.*

    a. mean that highways are closed   **b.** cause highways to be closed

11. She *whispered* to herself, "Sopa con jamón y cebollas."

    a. talked very quietly   **b.** thought very seriously

12. But even that misunderstanding *turned out all right in the end.*

    a. was OK after the plane turned back   **b.** had a happy ending

LOOKING AT SPECIAL EXPRESSIONS

Find the best way to complete each sentence. Write the letter of your answer on the line.

to head straight for = to go immediately to

1. He got on the bus and _____

2. When the children arrived at the park, _____

3. We were hungry, so when we got home, _____

    a. they headed straight for the playground.

    b. headed straight for the restroom.

    c. we headed straight for the kitchen.

by the time = when

4. By the time it reached the bus driver, _____

5. By the time I got home from the store, _____

6. By the time we got to the theater, _____

    d. the message was "There's a bomb in the rest room."

    e. the best seats were taken.

    f. the ice cream had melted.

The expression "in the world" is used with a question word to show surprise.

7. "No, I didn't get a plate," she answered, wondering _____

8. When the phone rang at 1 A.M. he wondered _____

9. When we told her we were going for a walk, she asked us _____

    g. why in the world we were going outside in such bad weather.

    h. who in the world would call at that hour.

    i. what in the world he meant.

no wonder = it's not surprising

10. No wonder the waiter didn't understand; _____

11. No wonder you're tired; _____

12. No wonder you didn't do well on the test; _____

    j. you didn't go to bed until after midnight last night.

    k. the woman had just ordered a very unusual lunch.

    l. you didn't study.

to feel like = to want to

13. The man who traveled to Auckland instead of Oakland _____

14. Let's go to the party; _____

15. I'll eat just a sandwich; _____

    m. didn't feel like laughing.

    n. I feel like dancing.

    o. I don't feel like eating a big dinner.

3. COMPREHENSION/READING SKILLS

UNDERSTANDING CAUSE AND EFFECT

Find the best way to complete each sentence. Write the letter of your answer on the line.

1. The man hid in the rest room _____

2. There was a 15-mile-long traffic jam _____

3. The man who wanted to fly to Oakland was worried _____

4. The Korean woman didn't ask her boss about his strange question _____

5. Her boss asked her, "Did you get up late?" _____

a. because the police closed the highway.

b. because he didn't want to pay for his bus ride.

c. because she had arrived at work fifteen minutes late.

d. because the plane seemed to be heading west, not north.

e. because she was too embarrassed.

UNDERSTANDING DETAILS

Read the sentences from the story. One word in each sentence is not correct. Find the word and cross it out. Write the correct word.

1. He had uncombed hair, dirty clothes, and only 35 dollars in his pocket.

2. In Baltimore, Maryland, he got on a train and headed straight for the rest room.

3. He thought that if he hid in the rest room, he could ride to Washington without paying.

4. But a driver at the back of the bus saw him.

5. She tapped the passenger in front of her on the foot and said, "There's a bum in the rest room."

Now copy three sentences from the story, but change one word in each sentence so that the information is not correct. Give your sentences to a classmate. Your classmate will find the incorrect word in each sentence, cross it out, and write the correct word. When your classmate is finished, check the corrections.

6. _____

_____

7. _____

_____

8. _____

_____

4. DISCUSSION

A. Think about these questions. Discuss your answers with your classmates.

1. In your country, if someone tried to ride a bus without paying, what do you think other passengers would do? What would you do?
2. Have you ever confused two similar-sounding English words? Which two words did you confuse? What happened?
3. In your native language, are there similar-sounding words (like *seventy* and *seventeen*) that people sometimes confuse? What are the words?

B. The message "There's a bum in the rest room" changed as people passed it to the front of the bus. Will a message that is passed around your classroom change, too? To find out, play the telephone game.

One of your classmates (Classmate 1) will whisper a message to a classmate sitting nearby (Classmate 2). The message can be anything, for example, "The weather is nice today, but tomorrow it's going to rain." Classmate 2 will whisper the message to Classmate 3. Classmate 3 will whisper the message to Classmate 4, and so on. (When a classmate whispers the message to you, you may not ask him or her to repeat it. You must pass the message you hear, even if it makes no sense.) The last classmate to hear the message will say it out loud. Is it the same message that Classmate 1 whispered?

5. WRITING

A. "I always wanted to see New Zealand," the man who flew to Auckland said. Is there a place that you've always wanted to see? Why do you want to go there? What sights do you want to see? Write about a place you've always wanted to visit.

B. The woman in the story ordered soup with soap and horses. Have you ever had a misunderstanding about food? Have you ever had a problem eating at someone's house, or buying food at a supermarket, or ordering food at a restaurant? Write about your experience. Here is what one student wrote.

On a visit to the United States, I went to a restaurant with my friends. I ordered a salad. The waitress asked me, "What kind of dressing do you want on your salad—blue cheese, ranch, Thousand Island, Italian, or French?" Of course, I said "French" because I am French. When the waitress brought the salad, I was shocked. The dressing was orange. I had never seen dressing like that in France. Then I tasted it. It tasted terrible. I never ordered "French" dressing again.

Challenge

Some English words and phrases sound so alike, they confuse even native speakers—people who have been speaking English all their lives.

Below are some mistakes that people in the United States—all native speakers—made. Which words did they confuse? Write your answer on the line.

(The words that people confused are listed side by side in the Answer Key. Ask a native speaker of English to read the words aloud. Can you hear any difference in the pronunciation?)

sauce	x-rayed	onion	ice cream
Youth in Asia	only	tennis shoes	messages
which it stands	self-esteem	a fried-egg	

1. A little boy asked his mother to make him a "Friday sandwich." The boy didn't really want a "Friday" between two slices of bread. He wanted _____ sandwich.

2. A teacher asked a seven-year-old girl if she had any brothers or sisters. "No," the girl answered. "I'm a lonely child." Actually, the expression isn't "a lonely child"; it's "an _____ child."

3. A young woman went to a movie with her boyfriend. As they were driving home, her boyfriend turned to her and said, "I'm going to take you to a place where they have the best diamond rings in the world." The woman was excited. Her boyfriend was going to buy her a diamond ring! A few minutes later, her boyfriend pulled into the drive-thru of a fast-food restaurant. When he ordered the food, the woman realized that her boyfriend hadn't said "the best diamond rings." He had said "the best _____ rings."

4. A little girl named Heather went to a Mexican restaurant with her family. When the waitress put Heather's dinner down in front of her, Heather covered her meal with her hands and told her parents, "Please don't put any hot socks on my food." Actually, it wasn't hot socks that Heather didn't like; it was hot _____.

5. A woman who hurt her arm went to the emergency room of a hospital. Doctors checked her arm and told her it was not badly hurt. After the woman left the hospital, a nurse wrote this on the woman's medical chart: "Patient was examined, X-rated, and sent home." Movies are sometimes X-rated, but patients are _____.

6. A teenaged girl wrote a letter to her girlfriend. She told her friend that her boyfriend had broken up with her, and now she didn't feel good about herself. She wrote that he hurt her "self of steam." Actually, the expression "self of steam" doesn't exist in English. She meant to say that the boy had hurt her _____.

7. A teacher asked her students to name famous Americans in history. One boy replied, "Richard Stans." The teacher was puzzled. She had never heard of Richard Stans. "Who is he?" she asked the boy. "I'm not sure," the boy answered, "but he must be very important. Every morning we all stand and face the flag. Then we say, 'I pledge allegiance to the flag of the United States of America, and to the republic for Richard Stans.'" The teacher had to laugh. The boy had misunderstood the correct words, which are: "I pledge allegiance to the flag of the United States of America, and to the republic for _____."

8. A large department store had an optical department where people could get eye exams and buy glasses. One day the optical department was giving free eye exams. So, this was announced over the store's public address system: "The optical department is giving a free eye screening today." A lot of people who were shopping at the store heard the announcement and hurried to the optical department, where a long line formed. It turned out, however, that the people weren't waiting for a free eye screening; they were waiting for free _____.

9. High school students who took a public speaking class had to give a speech. One student chose as her topic euthanasia—the painless killing of people who are incurably sick. After she gave her speech, one student said to another, "Her speech was interesting. But she didn't say anything about teenagers in countries like Japan and China." The student thought the topic of the speech was not "Euthanasia" but "_____."

10. A magazine advertised over the radio. The magazine offered a special price of $19.95 for a subscription. For $19.95, people would receive ten issues of the magazine. When some people called the magazine's toll-free number to place their orders, they gave their credit card numbers and then their shoe sizes. Why did they give their shoe sizes? The people had misunderstood the words "ten issues." They thought they were ordering

_____.

UNIT 7

1. PRE-READING

Look at the picture and think about these questions. Discuss your answers with your classmates.

- What is a thrift store?
- In your native country, do you have thrift stores or other places where you can buy things cheaply? Describe them to your classmates.
- The men in the picture are looking at something that one of the men bought at a thrift store. What do you think it is? Why do you think the man on the right looks so happy?

A Real Bargain

A few years ago Ed Jones was shopping at a thrift store in Indianapolis, Indiana. He walked past the used clothing and stopped at the used books. He looked at the books and then at some old dishes. Mr. Jones was looking for something that might be valuable. If he found something valuable, he would buy it cheaply and then resell it, perhaps to an antique dealer. But today Mr. Jones didn't see anything he wanted, so he started walking toward the door. Then something caught his eye. Leaning against a wall there was a large cardboard map.

Mr. Jones walked over for a closer look. The map was covered with dust, so Mr. Jones wiped it with his handkerchief. Under the dust was a color map of Paris. It looked old. On the back of the map, someone had written the price: $3. Mr. Jones was quite certain that the map was worth more than three dollars, so he bought it. He thought he could probably sell it for $40.

Later, at home, Mr. Jones looked more closely at the map. He decided it might be very old. Maybe it was worth even more than $40.

The next day Mr. Jones took the map to a geography professor at a nearby university. The professor was a map expert. After looking at the map for a few minutes, he became very excited. "I've read about this map!" he exclaimed. Then he told Mr. Jones what he knew.

In 1671 the king of France, Louis XIV, asked a cartographer to make a map of Paris. The cartographer worked on the map for four years. The map he drew was beautiful—it was not just a map, but a work of art as well. The cartographer made several black and white copies of the map. Then he carefully colored one of the copies, using blue for rivers, green for trees, and brown for buildings. The professor said that one black and white copy of the map was in the British Museum in London, and another was in the Bibliotheque Nationale in Paris. "I think," the professor told Mr. Jones, "that you've just found the color copy of the map—in a thrift store in Indianapolis!" The professor suggested that Mr. Jones take the map to New York City. Experts there could tell Mr. Jones if the professor was right.

The New York experts said the professor *was* right. They told Mr. Jones that he had the only color copy of the map and that it was extremely valuable. "How much do you think it's worth?" Mr. Jones asked the experts. "Millions," they replied. "It's impossible to say exactly how much the map is worth. It's worth whatever someone is willing to pay for it."

Soon Mr. Jones discovered how much people were willing to pay for the map. Someone offered him 10 million dollars; then someone else immediately offered him 12 million. The most recent offer was 19.5 million dollars. Mr. Jones hasn't decided whether he will sell his three-dollar map at that price or wait for a higher offer. He is thinking it over.

But how in the world did this map find its way to a thrift store in Indianapolis? Here is what some experts think: The map was probably in a museum or in the home of a wealthy family in France. Then a thief stole it, perhaps during the confusion of World War I or World War II. The thief sold the map to an antique dealer in France. The French antique dealer, not knowing how valuable the map was, sold it to an antique dealer in Indianapolis. That antique dealer, who also did not know its value, gave it to a neighbor. For ten years the map hung on a wall in the neighbor's house. Then the neighbor got tired of it and sold it to the thrift store. The map sat in the thrift store for months. Finally, Mr. Jones discovered it.

When Mr. Jones went shopping at the thrift store, he was looking for a bargain. He wanted to find something that was worth more than the price he paid. He paid three dollars for the map, and it is worth at least 19.5 million dollars. Now *that's* a bargain!

2. VOCABULARY

LOOKING AT THE STORY

Which words have the same meanings as the words in the story? Circle the letter of the correct answer.

1. Ed Jones was shopping at a *thrift store*.
   a. store that sells used things at low prices
   b. store that sells expensive things at high prices

2. If he found something valuable, he could resell it, perhaps to an *antique dealer*.
   a. person who fixes broken things
   b. a person who buys and sells old things

3. Leaning against a wall of the store there was a large *cardboard* map.
   a. made of heavy paper
   b. made of plastic

4. Mr. Jones was quite *certain* that the map was worth more than three dollars.
   a. worried
   b. sure

5. The next day Mr. Jones took the map to a *geography* professor at a nearby university.
   a. the study of the world's countries, cities, oceans, rivers, and mountains
   b. the study of the world's history, languages, and customs

6. "I've read about this map!" he *exclaimed*.
   a. said with strong feeling
   b. said very quietly

7. Louis XIV asked a *cartographer* to make a map of Paris.
   a. person who draws maps
   b. person who writes books

8. The New York experts told Mr. Jones that his map was *extremely* valuable.
   a. not really
   b. very

9. "How much do you think it's worth?" Mr. Jones asked the experts. "Millions," they *replied*.
   a. answered
   b. asked

10. Someone *offered him ten million dollars*.
    a. said, "Will you take ten million dollars for the map?"
    b. told him, "I think your map is worth ten million dollars."

11. Some experts think the map was probably in a museum or in the home of a *wealthy* family in France.
    a. famous
    b. rich

12. When Mr. Jones went shopping at the thrift store, he was looking for a *bargain*.
    a. something that can be bought cheaply
    b. something that has been used

LOOKING AT SPECIAL EXPRESSIONS

Find the best way to complete each sentence. Write the letter of your answer on the line.

to catch one's eye = to get one's attention

1. Mr. Jones was walking toward the door _____

2. She was leaving the museum _____

3. He was walking through the department store _____

a. when a painting by Renoir caught her eye.

b. when a large cardboard map caught his eye.

c. when a sweater caught his eye.

to be worth = to have a value of

4. Mr. Jones was quite certain that _____

5. They paid $100,000 for their house, but _____

6. He tried to sell his old TV for $500, but nobody bought it because _____

d. the map was worth more than three dollars.

e. it wasn't worth more than $250.

f. it was worth at least $125,000.

because to be willing to = to be ready to

7. The map was worth whatever _____

8. Our teacher said that _____

9. I won't have to take the bus home because _____

g. he was willing to give us extra help after class.

h. my friend is willing to give me a ride.

i. someone was willing to pay for it.

to get tired of = to become no longer interested in

10. The neighbor got tired of the map and _____

11. He got tired of hamburgers _____

12. I'm getting tired of studying French; _____

j. after eating them every day for a month.

k. sold it to a thrift store.

l. maybe I'll study Spanish next year.

3. COMPREHENSION/READING SKILLS

UNDERSTANDING CAUSE AND EFFECT

Find the best way to complete each sentence. Write the letter of your answer on the line.

1. Ed Jones went to the thrift store _____

2. He wiped the map with his handkerchief _____

3. The professor suggested that Mr. Jones take the map to New York City _____

4. Experts in New York said the map was extremely valuable _____

5. The map was a bargain _____

a. because experts there could tell Mr. Jones if the professor was right.

b. because it was cheap but very valuable.

c. because he was looking for a bargain.

d. because it was the only color copy.

e. because it was covered with dust.

UNDERSTANDING DETAILS

Read the sentences from the story. One word in each sentence is not correct. Find the word and cross it out. Write the correct word.

1. The map was covered with paint.

2. Under the dust Mr. Jones found a color map of Rome.

3. The map looked new.

4. On the back of the map, someone had written the price: $30.

5. The next day Mr. Jones took the map to a mathematics professor at the university.

Now copy three sentences from the story, but change one word in each sentence so that the information is not correct. Give your sentences to a classmate. Your classmate will find the incorrect word in each sentence, cross it out, and write the correct word. When your classmate is finished, check the corrections.

6. _____

_____

7. _____

_____

8. _____

_____

4. DISCUSSION

A. Think about these questions. Discuss your answers with your classmates.

  1. After reading the story, do you think you might go to a thrift store to look for something valuable?

  2. Have you—or has anyone you know—ever had an experience similar to Mr. Jones's experience? Have you ever bought something at a low price and then discovered it was worth more than you paid for it? Have you ever had the opposite experience? Have you ever bought something at a high price and then discovered that it was worth less than you paid for it?

B. Be a cartographer. Draw a map of a country you know. Put important rivers, mountains, cities, and tourist attractions on the map. Then show your map to a classmate. Tell your classmate about the places on your map.

5. WRITING

A. What would you do if, like Mr. Jones, you suddenly had 19.5 million dollars? How would you use the money? Make a list of what you would do.

1. _____

_____

2. _____

_____

3. _____

_____

4. _____

_____

5. _____

_____

B. Imagine that you went to a thrift store and bought something cheaply. The object could be jewelry, a book, a painting, a photograph, a toy, a vase—or anything else that you want it to be. Imagine that later you discovered that the object you bought is very valuable—that it's worth much, much more than you paid for it.

Write a story. In the story, describe what you bought, tell what it's really worth, and explain why it's valuable. Here is what one student wrote.

I bought a dress at a thrift store. It was red and made of lace. It was only one dollar.

I wore the dress to a party. A woman at the party stared at me for a long time. Then she asked me, "Where did you get that dress?" "I got it from a friend," I answered. That was not true, but I didn't want to say that I had bought it at a thrift store for only one dollar. "That was Miss K's dress," the woman said. "She wore it at her last concert." (Miss K was a famous singer.) "I'm a great fan of Miss K," the woman continued. "I have all her CDs, and I have many photographs of her. But I don't have anything that she wore. Will you please sell me that dress? I don't know what your friend paid for it, but I'm willing to pay $500."

I told her she could have the dress for $500 and went home from the party very happy.

Challenge

Ed Jones' three-dollar map is worth at least 19.5 million dollars. Can you guess what the items below are worth? All of these valuable items were sold at Christie's Auction House in New York. The most valuable item sold for 3.5 million dollars. The least valuable item sold for $38,000.

Read the descriptions of the items. Then take a guess: which item do you think sold for 3.5 million dollars? Which one do you think sold for $38,000?

Letter Handwritten by Abraham Lincoln

Abraham Lincoln was president of the United States during the Civil War (1861–1865), when the Southern states fought the Northern states over the issue of slavery. The Southern states wanted to separate from the United States.

When the Civil War began, a man named William McCullough wanted to fight for the North. The army rejected him because he was blind in one eye. McCullough had once worked for Lincoln, and he asked the president for help. President Lincoln intervened, and the army accepted McCullough. He was killed in battle.

McCullough's daughter, Fanny, was distraught over her father's death, and Lincoln wrote her a letter of condolence. He comforted Fanny with these words: "You cannot now realize that you will ever feel better. Is this not so? And yet it is a mistake. You are sure to be happy again. To know this, which is certainly true, will make your sorrow less miserable now. I have had experience enough to know what I say; and you need only to believe it, to feel better now."

This is one of Lincoln's most famous letters. It is considered to be one of the greatest condolence letters ever written.

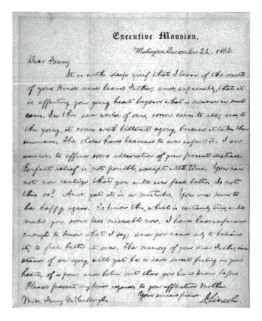

Andy Warhol Painting

The painter Andy Warhol was one of the most influential artists of the twentieth century. He died in New York City in 1987.

Warhol's style of painting is called Pop Art because he took popular, common images and transformed them into art. He painted Coca-Cola bottles, U.S. one-dollar bills, the faces of movie stars, and soup cans. He is perhaps most famous for his soup-can paintings, which he completed in 1961 and 1962. There are thirty-two paintings of soup cans, and each painting is slightly different. This painting is of Campbell's "Pepper Pot" soup.

Steiff Teddy Bear

Margarete Steiff, a German woman, created the first teddy bear over 100 years ago. Ms. Steiff wasn't originally a toy maker; she was a seamstress who fell into toy making by chance.

Margarete had polio as an infant, and she was never able to walk. So, when she became a young woman, she needed to find work she could do while sitting in a wheelchair. She decided to become a seamstress. By the time she was twenty-five, Margarete was earning a good living making dresses for wealthy women.

One day Margarete was looking through a fashion magazine and spotted a pattern for a toy elephant made of cloth. She made several elephants and gave them to friends as gifts. Her friends loved their toy elephants and encouraged Margarete to make more cloth toys. She began making little bears, dogs, and donkeys and selling them, in addition to selling dresses.

By 1897 Margarete was selling more toys than dresses; in fact, she was selling so many toys, she had to hire forty women to help her sew them. The most popular toys were the cloth bears. In the United States, the bears were an instant hit. They were called "teddy bears" after President Theodore Roosevelt, whose nickname was Teddy.

The Steiff Company is still in business in Germany. New Steiff teddy bears are quite expensive because they are made by hand. It is the old teddy bears, however—the ones that Margarete Steiff and her forty employees made—that are really valuable. This Steiff teddy bear, which was made in 1905, is in almost perfect condition.

Diana's Blue Velvet Dress

In 1997, Diana, Princess of Wales, decided to auction some of her evening dresses and to give the money to charity. The auction was held at Christie's Auction House in New York City in June, two months before her death. On the evening of the auction, the auction house was packed with people, and fifty telephone lines connected the auction to bidders all over the world.

That evening this blue velvet evening gown brought the highest price. Princess Diana had worn the dress to a dinner at the White House with U.S. President Ronald Reagan and his wife, Nancy. Princess Diana was a fan of Hollywood movies, so the Reagans invited several movie stars to the dinner. After dinner, Diana danced with one of her favorite actors, John Travolta. The next morning, newspapers all over the world carried photos of Diana dancing in her blue velvet gown.

Check the Answer Key to see how much these items sold for.

Unit 8

1. PRE-READING

Are you superstitious? Read the sentences. Then check (✔) "yes" or "no."

	Yes	No
1. Black cats are unlucky.	____	____
2. It is unlucky to break a mirror.	____	____
3. If I point at the moon, something bad will happen to me.	____	____
4. It is bad luck when a shoelace breaks.	____	____
5. If my palm itches, I will receive money.	____	____
6. When I want good luck, I sometimes cross my fingers or knock on wood.	____	____
7. I have a lucky number.	____	____
8. I have something that I consider lucky—a lucky pen or a lucky hat, for example.	____	____

If you checked "yes" after any of these statements, you are probably a little superstitious.

Who in your class is superstitious?
Who in your class is not superstitious?

Black Cats and Broken Mirrors

Do you think that it is bad luck to walk under a ladder or break a mirror? Do you think that black cats and the number 13 are unlucky? The three men in the picture don't. Every Friday the 13th they walk under ladders, break mirrors, and open umbrellas indoors. They want to prove that they aren't at all superstitious. They may be the only people in the world who aren't. There are over one million superstitions, and most people believe at least one or two of them.

Many people are superstitious about numbers. They think that there are lucky numbers and unlucky numbers. The number 13 is often considered unlucky. In some parts of the world, buildings have no 13th floor and streets have no houses with the number 13. In Japan, 4 is considered unlucky because in Japanese the word "four" is pronounced the same as the word "death." Japanese never give gifts of four knives, four napkins, or four of anything. What are the lucky numbers? Seven is a lucky number in many places, and 8 is considered lucky in Japan and China. In China, businesses often open on August 8 (8-8), and many couples register to get married at eight past eight on August 8.

Superstitions about numbers are so widespread that some people—called numerologists—make a living giving advice about numbers. In 1937, when the Toyoda family of Japan wanted to form a car company, they asked a numerologist if "Toyoda" would be a good name for the company. The numerologist said it would not be. He explained that "Toyoda" took ten strokes of the pen to write, and 10 was not a lucky number. "Toyota," however, took eight strokes to write, and eight was a very lucky number. The numerologist recommended "Toyota" as a better name for the company. The family took his advice. As a result, millions of people drive "Toyotas" and not "Toyodas."

In addition to superstitions about numbers, there are many other kinds of superstitions. There are superstitions about eating, sleeping, sneezing, and itching. There are superstitions about animals and holidays and horseshoes. There are even superstitions about superstitions. Those superstitions tell people how to reverse bad luck.

For example, in many parts of the world spilling salt is bad luck. Throwing salt, however, is good luck. So, people who spill salt throw a little of the spilled salt over their left shoulder. Throwing the spilled salt reverses the bad luck. When the Japanese bump heads, they immediately bump heads again. According to a Japanese superstition, the first bump means their parents will die, but the second bump "erases" the first bump. To reverse bad luck in general, people turn around three times, turn their pockets inside out, or put their hats on backward. In the United States, baseball players sometimes wear their caps backward when their team is losing. It looks silly, but the baseball players don't mind if it helps them win the game.

Because there are so many superstitions, it is not surprising that some of them are contradictory. In Germany, it is good luck when the left eye twitches and bad luck when the right eye twitches. In Malaysia, it is exactly the opposite: a twitching right eye means good luck, and a twitching left eye means bad luck. Accidentally putting on clothes inside out brings good luck in Pakistan but bad luck in Costa Rica. In Chile, unmarried people won't take the last piece of food on the plate because it means they will never marry. In Thailand, unmarried people take the last piece because it means they will marry someone good-looking.

Some superstitions have been with us for so long that they have become customs. In many parts of the world it is polite to say "Health" or "God bless you" when someone sneezes. People used to think that the soul could escape from the body during a sneeze. They said "God bless you" to protect people from losing their souls. Today we no longer believe that people who sneeze are in danger of losing their souls, but we say "God bless you" anyway. We say it not because we are superstitious, but because we are polite.

Even people who say they aren't superstitious would probably not do what the men in the picture do—intentionally walk under ladders and break mirrors. Almost everyone is at least a little superstitious. One woman says that when she got married, her aunt gave her white bath towels. "Never buy purple towels," her aunt said. "If you use purple towels, your marriage will end." Does the woman believe that superstition? "No, of course not," she says. "It's silly." Does she use purple towels? "Well, no," she answers. "Why take chances?"

2. VOCABULARY

LOOKING AT THE STORY

Which words or picture has the same meaning as the words in the reading selection? Circle the letter of the correct answer.

1. Do you think that it is bad luck to walk under a *ladder?*
   a. (In the photo on page 58, the man in the center is standing under it.)
   b. (In the photo on page 58, the man on the right is standing under it.)

2. The men walk under ladders and break mirrors to *prove* that they aren't superstitious.
   a. believe it is crazy
   b. show it is true

3. Superstitions about numbers are *widespread.*
   a. found in many places
   b. believed only by children

4. Some people *make a living* giving people advice about numbers.
   a. make money
   b. make mistakes

5. "Toyota" took *eight strokes* of the pen to write.

   a.
   b.

6. The family *took his advice.*
   a. did what he suggested
   b. asked for more information

7. There are superstitions that *reverse bad luck.*
   a. change bad luck to good luck
   b. give the bad luck to someone else

8. If you *spill salt,* immediately throw a little of the spilled salt over your left shoulder.
   a. use too much salt
   b. pour out salt accidentally

9. It looks silly, but *the baseball players don't mind* if it helps them win the game.
   a. that's OK with the baseball players
   b. the baseball players don't like to think about it

10. Some superstitions *are contradictory.* In Germany, it is good luck when the left eye twitches. In Malaysia, it is bad luck when the left eye twitches.
    a. are very old
    b. mean the opposite

11. Putting clothes on *inside out* brings good luck in Pakistan.
    a. in the house, rather than outside
    b. with the inside parts on the outside

12. People used to think that the soul could *escape* from the body during a sneeze.
    a. enter
    b. leave

LOOKING AT SPECIAL EXPRESSIONS

Find the best way to complete each sentence. Write the letter of your answer on the line.

as a result = because of that

1. The family took the numerologist's advice. As a result, _____

2. He overslept. As a result, _____

3. She didn't study; as a result, _____

in addition to = as well as ("In addition to" connects two similar ideas.)

4. In addition to the superstitions about numbers, _____

5. In addition to studying French, _____

6. In addition to being an excellent student, _____

according to Mr. Jones = Mr. Jones says that

7. According to a Japanese superstition, _____

8. According to my watch, _____

9. According to this map, _____

a. he was late for work.

b. she didn't do well on the test.

c. millions of people today drive "Toyotas" and not "Toyodas."

d. she is an excellent dancer and swimmer.

e. there are many other kinds of superstitions.

f. he is studying German and Spanish.

g. the museum is on Michigan Avenue.

h. bumping heads means your parents will die.

i. it's a quarter to nine.

3. COMPREHENSION/READING SKILLS

UNDERSTANDING THE MAIN IDEAS

What information is *not* in the story? Draw a line through the three sentences with information that is not in the story.

- The men in the picture want to prove they are not superstitious.
- There are over one million superstitions.
- Children are usually not superstitious.
- Many people are superstitious about numbers.
- Numerologists make a living giving people advice about numbers.
- It is always a good idea to take a numerologist's advice.
- Some superstitions tell people how to reverse bad luck.
- Some superstitions are contradictory.
- Some superstitions have become customs.
- People who use purple towels are silly.
- Almost everyone is at least a little superstitious.

UNDERSTANDING SUPPORTING DETAILS

Find the best way to complete each sentence. Write the letter of your answer on the line.

1. Many people are superstitious about numbers. For example, _____

2. Some people—called numerologists— make a living giving people advice about numbers. For example, _____

3. There are superstitions that tell people how to reverse bad luck. For example, _____

4. Some superstitions are contradictory. For example, _____

5. Some superstitions have been with us for so long that they have become customs. For example, _____

a. accidentally putting on clothes inside out brings good luck in Pakistan but bad luck in Costa Rica.

b. it is polite to say "Health" or "God bless you" when someone sneezes.

c. throwing spilled salt over the left shoulder reverses bad luck.

d. the number 13 is often considered unlucky.

e. a numerologist recommended "Toyota" as a name for the car company.

4. DISCUSSION

Form small conversation groups. Ask the people in your group if they know any superstitions about:

salt	rabbits	eye twitching	sleeping
ladders	elephants	shivering	dreams
mirrors	horseshoes	whistling	leaving the house
brooms	garlic	cutting nails	finding a coin
combs	four-leaf clovers	taking photos	opening an umbrella
knives	numbers	giving gifts	knocking on wood
shoes	hiccups	cooking	weddings
black cats	itching	eating a pear	New Year's Day
crows	sneezing	dropping silverware	funeral processions
owls	ears ringing	chopsticks	

5. WRITING

A. Make a list of superstitions that some people in your country believe. Here is an example from a student from Panama:

1. Always sleep with your feet facing the door of your room.
2. If you give your sweetheart a handkerchief or socks, you will argue.
3. If you want a visitor to leave, turn your broom upside down.
4. If a young woman is sweeping the floor and the broom accidentally touches her feet, she will marry a rich old man.
5. To protect yourself from evil spirits, wear your pajamas inside out.

B. Write about something you have that is lucky—a lucky number or a lucky hat, for example. Why is it lucky? Can you remember a time when it brought you good luck? Here is what one student wrote.

When I was a high school student, I had a difficult mathematics test one day. Before the test our teacher told us, "Use the same pencil you used when you studied last night. When you can't solve a problem, hold the pencil tightly. If you do that, you will be able to solve the problem." I did that, and I got every answer right. I thought, "This is my lucky pencil." But later I discovered that my pencil was lucky only sometimes. When I studied hard, my pencil helped me, but when I didn't study hard, it didn't help me.

C. Has there ever been a time when you've had very good—or very bad—luck? Write about it. Here is what one student wrote.

Last month I had a very unlucky day. I overslept in the morning because I had forgotten to set my alarm clock. It was raining. On the way to the bus stop I fell and got wet. Then I missed the bus and was late for my class.

That night a friend of mine called me while I was cooking dinner. It was a long phone call, and I forgot about my dinner. When I finished talking to my friend, I went into the kitchen to check on my dinner. It was burned. I thought, "I have only two hands and one head. I'm trying to do too much." But later I thought, "I was just not lucky today."

Challenge

Many superstitions and customs that are common in the United States are actually thousands of years old. They have their origins in ancient beliefs.

Read about these ancient beliefs. Then match each ancient belief with a modern superstition or custom from page 65. Write the letter of your answer on the line.

Long ago . . .

1. The people who lived in present-day Europe believed that gods lived in trees. Perhaps they came to this conclusion because lightning often strikes trees. Or perhaps they saw trees losing their leaves in the autumn and growing new leaves in the spring and thought that gods and goddesses inside the trees were making these seasonal changes. At any rate, ancient people believed that trees (especially oak trees) had divine power. When people had a favor to ask, they knocked on a tree to let the resident god know they were there and then made their request. If the request was granted, they returned to the tree and knocked a few times to say "thank you." _____

2. The ancient Greeks had many gods and goddesses. The goddess of the moon, marriage, and childbirth was Artemis. On Artemis's birthday, people baked moon-shaped cakes and brought them to Artemis's temple. They also brought candles to the temple and placed them on the altars there. All the candles were lit and then blown out at the same time. If the people blew out all the candles in one communal breath, Artemis was happy with her worshipers. If some candles remained lit, Artemis was unhappy. _____

3. In ancient Asia, people who were sentenced to death were hung. Sometimes they were hung from trees, and sometimes they were hung from the seventh rung of a ladder that was placed against a building. People believed that the space under a ladder that had been used for a hanging was dangerous because the spirit of the dead man could linger there long after the body was gone. _____

4. An ancient legend goes something like this: A king with three daughters asks each one to describe how much she loves him. The oldest daughter says she loves him as much as bread. The middle daughter says she loves him as much as wine. The youngest daughter says she loves him as much as salt. The king is furious that his youngest daughter compared her love for him with her love for salt, and he says she must leave the palace. She leaves, but secretly she meets with the palace cook. She asks the cook to leave salt out of her father's meals. The king realizes the importance of salt and calls his youngest daughter back. This story was told by the Romans 2,000 years ago. Salt was important not only to them, but to people throughout the ancient world. It was used to preserve and flavor food, and it was so valuable, it was considered almost supernatural. _____

5. Two thousand years ago, the Etruscans—people who lived in what is now central Italy— used chickens to tell the future. The Etruscans would draw a circle on the ground, divide the circle into sections—one section for each letter of the alphabet—and put kernels of corn in each section. Then they put a chicken in the circle and observed the chicken as it picked up corn. For example, if a young woman wanted to know the first letter of her future husband's name, she would ask that question and then watch to see which section of the circle the chicken went to. After the chicken did its work, it was killed and its collarbone was hung out to dry. Two people then made a wish on the bone. One person held on to one end of the bone while another person held on to the other end.

Then both people pulled. When the bone broke, the person left holding the larger piece got his or her wish. (This was called the "lucky break.") _____

6. Between the Middle Ages and the eighteenth century, witch hunts were common in Europe. People believed they had to find witches and kill them, for witches had the power to do great harm. The suspected "witches" were typically old women who were eccentric and who lived alone. Old women who had cats were especially feared because people believed that cats could be demons who had taken the shape of a cat. The fear of witches eventually subsided, but fear of cats—particularly black cats—remained.

_____

7. Ancient people believed that evil spirits were everywhere, waiting for opportunities to harm people. The spirits were attracted particularly to weddings, where it was easy for them to spot two happy young people—the bride and the groom—and give them bad luck. There was, however, a way to outsmart the evil spirits. Friends of the bride dressed exactly as she was dressed, and friends of the groom dressed exactly as he was dressed. That way the evil spirits wouldn't know who was getting married. _____

In the United States today . . .

a. At weddings, the bridesmaids—friends of the bride—wear identical dresses and the grooms men—friends of the groom—wear identical suits.

b. When people talk about their good fortune, they knock on wood to protect their good luck.

c. It is considered unlucky to spill salt, and people who spill it immediately throw a little of the spilled salt over their left shoulders to reverse the bad luck. (They throw the salt over their left shoulders because primitive people believed that evil spirits were always on the left.)

d. People believe it is bad luck if a black cat crosses their path.

e. People bake birthday cakes which they top with candles. The person celebrating a birthday tries to blow out all the candles in one breath for good luck.

f. People are afraid to walk under a ladder.

g. After eating a chicken, people dry the collarbone, which is called the "wishbone." Two people make a wish and pull on the bone. After the bone breaks, the person holding the larger piece gets his or her wish.

UNIT 9

1. PRE-READING

Look at the picture and think about these questions. Discuss your answers with your classmates.

- Do you like stories that scare you?
- Do you know a scary story? Tell it to your classmates.
- Is your scary story true, or not true? How do you know?

A Killer in the Backseat

Have you heard this story?

At two A.M., a young nurse left the hospital where she worked, got into her car, and headed for home. On the way home, she stopped at an all-night store for milk. As she was paying for the milk, the cashier reminded her to be careful. "You know about the murder, don't you?" he asked her.

Of course she knew about the murder. A few weeks before, a local woman who had been driving alone late at night had been murdered. The police were still looking for the killer.

The woman got into her car, locked the car doors, and pulled out of the parking lot. A man in a pickup truck pulled out right behind her and followed her, staying just inches from her rear bumper. Every few seconds, he turned on his bright lights.

Her heart pounding, the woman sped home. When she pulled into her driveway, the man in the pickup truck pulled in right behind her. The woman threw open the car door and ran toward her house. Halfway to the front door, she fainted.

When the woman came to, she saw a man kneeling beside her. He was the man in the pickup truck! "It's OK," the man said and pointed to another man lying on the ground nearby. The man's hands and feet were tied.

"I'm the one who followed you," the stranger said. "I had just pulled into the parking lot of the all-night store when I saw a man get into your car and crouch down in the backseat. Then you came out of the store and got into the car. There was nothing I could do but follow you. I turned on my bright lights every time the guy popped up from the backseat to let him know I was behind you. When you got out of your car, he tried to run away. I hit him with my tire iron. He had a knife, but he didn't get a chance to use it. The police are on their way here. I'm sorry I scared you."

"That's all right," the woman said. "That's all right."

It is a frightening story, and it could have happened. It *could* have happened, but it didn't. It is an urban legend.

Urban legends, like ancient legends, are stories that people tell one another. They are called urban legends because they often take place in or near cities.

Urban legends are not true stories, but many people believe they are true because they are very realistic. Sometimes urban legends are so believable, they are picked up by the media and reported as news. If urban legends fool even experienced news reporters, how can the average person know if a story is true, or if it is an urban legend?

An urban legend always has this characteristic: It is a friend-of-a-friend story. Someone telling an urban legend might begin, "This really happened to my hairdresser's son-in-law," or "Did you hear what happened to my neighbor's cousin?" But if you try to trace the story back to the son-in-law or the cousin, the trail always evaporates.

Another characteristic of an urban legend is that it is rich in detail. An urban legend always includes the names of local people, local places, and local streets. For example, a person telling the story of the killer in the backseat would never begin, "A young nurse left the hospital where she worked." Instead, the story would begin something like this:

"You know Mr. Soto—the man who lives next door to my cousin? Well, this really happened to his niece. She works at Community Hospital. Anyway, last week she was on her way home from work, about two in the morning, and. . . ."

As an urban legend moves from person to person, and from city to city, the details of the story change. Mr. Soto's niece becomes Mrs. Alberti's daughter-in-law. She isn't a nurse at Community Hospital; she's a waitress at the Coffee Cup Cafe. The story, though, remains essentially the same, no matter how far it travels. And these days, urban legends do indeed travel far.

In the past, urban legends spread by word of mouth—one person told the story to another person. Now urban legends spread by phone, fax, and E-mail. They spread to every corner of the world, and with lightning speed.

One final story.

This book—*Even More True Stories*—has magical powers. On the front cover of the book, there is a symbol that looks like this:

If you put your hand on the symbol and make a wish, your wish will come true. One student put her hand on the symbol and wished for a lot of money. The next day, she won the lottery—six million dollars. This really happened. The student who won the lottery is the sister of my nephew's girlfriend.

2. VOCABULARY

LOOKING AT THE STORY

Write the correct word or words on the line.

came to	detail	essentially	headed	reminded
spread by word of mouth	fool	rear bumper	realistic	

1. The cashier wanted the nurse to remember that a woman had been killed. He _____ her about the murder.

2. After the woman bought milk, she went in the direction of her house. She _____ for home.

3. The man in the pickup truck was behind the woman's car. He stayed just inches from her _____.

4. The woman fainted. A few minutes later, she woke up. When she _____, she saw a man kneeling beside her.

5. Urban legends are believable stories that could happen in real life. Urban legends are very _____.

6. The media sometimes make mistakes and they report urban legends as news. Urban legends _____ even experienced reporters.

7. Urban legends always include the names of local people, places, and streets; they are rich in _____.

8. Details in an urban legend change as the story moves from city to city, but the main events of the story don't change. The story remains _____ the same.

9. Urban legends _____—one person tells the story to another person.

LOOKING AT SPECIAL EXPRESSIONS

Find the best way to complete each sentence. Write the letter of your answer on the line.

to pull in
to pull into = to enter (while driving a car)
to pull onto

1. The woman sped home and _____   **a.** take your umbrella.

2. It's going to rain; you'd better _____   **b.** pulled into her driveway.

3. When we got a flat tire, we _____   **c.** pulled onto the shoulder of the road.

to let someone know = to tell someone; to inform

4. The man in the pickup truck turned on his bright lights _____

d. please let everyone know it's at one o'clock, not two.

5. If you need any help fixing your car, _____

e. just let me know; I've worked as a mechanic.

6. We've changed the time of the meeting; _____

f. to let the man in the backseat know he saw him.

no matter how = it makes no difference.

7. No matter how far an urban legend travels, _____

g. he doesn't gain weight because he exercises a lot.

8. No matter how much he eats, _____

h. we have to finish this job.

9. No matter how long it takes, _____

i. the story remains essentially the same.

3. COMPREHENSION/READING SKILLS

UNDERSTANDING THE MAIN IDEAS

Check (✔) six correct ways to complete the sentence.

Urban legends . . .

_____ are not true.

_____ are ancient.

_____ often take place in or near cities.

_____ are realistic.

_____ are friend-of-a-friend stories.

_____ have many details.

_____ always include the names of famous people.

_____ remain essentially the same, no matter how far they travel.

UNDERSTANDING CAUSE AND EFFECT

Find the best way to complete each sentence. Write the letter of your answer on the line.

1. Untrue stories that people tell one another are called urban legends _____

2. Urban legends are sometimes reported as news _____

3. A story that begins, "This really happened to my neighbor's cousin" might be an urban legend _____

4. Urban legends move from city to city, yet still include the names of local people and local places _____

5. These days, urban legends travel fast _____

a. because the storytellers change the details to fit the city.

b. because they spread not only by word of mouth, but by fax and E-mail.

c. because it has a friend-of-a-friend beginning.

d. because they are very believable.

e. because they often take place in or near cities.

4. DISCUSSION

Below are topics of some popular urban legends. Have you heard the story? (If not, what do you think the story might be?) Tell the class. (If you're curious about these urban legends, you can read many of them on the Internet. Type "urban legend" and let your search engine take you to the urban legend web sites.)

- a restaurant that serves dog (or cat or rat) meat
- a mouse in a can of soda
- a young woman who is kidnapped from a dressing room in a department store (She falls through a trap door.)
- looking into a mirror and seeing ghosts or a woman with no eyes
- a poisonous snake in an imported blanket (or sweater or coat)
- a carpet layer who sees a bump in a carpet and finds a missing pet canary (or hamster or gerbil)
- a hitchhiker who disappears
- a female hitchhiker with hairy arms or the feet of a horse
- a tourist from the United States who asks the taxi driver (or tour guide), "How long did it take to build it?" every time he sees a famous building
- a dead rabbit that is shampooed and dried with a hair dryer
- tourists in Australia who put a coat on a kangaroo
- a European couple who go to a restaurant in Hong Kong with their little dog, who is hungry
- a female insect that goes into someone's ear
- a grandmother who dies on a family vacation
- spiders in a cactus or yucca plant
- a stolen kidney
- stolen children
- a baby-sitter who gets a phone call from a killer
- a rich man who gives a reward to someone who helps him when his limousine breaks down on the highway
- drug dealers who give children colorful stickers

5. WRITING

Rewrite the "Killer in the Backseat" story, or one of the stories your classmates told in the Discussion exercise. Give the story the characteristics of an urban legend: make it a "friend-of-a-friend" story; add details; and include the names of local people, places, and streets. This is what one student wrote.

A friend of my mom's friend is a taxi driver in Sao Paulo, Brazil. Her name is Monica. Like many taxi drivers, Monica has amazing stories. The story I'm going to tell you now is true. This really happened to Monica.

Monica was driving her taxi home after a long day. At exactly midnight she was passing Primavera Cemetery and saw a woman in a black dress holding her arm out for a taxi. She stopped the taxi, and the woman got in the back seat. She introduced herself as Carol. Carol said that her car had broken down. Carol asked Monica to drive her to her parents' house on Boa Vista Street. The whole trip, Carol asked weird questions about death. Sometimes Monica looked back at Carol just to see her face, but it was too dark and she couldn't see it. Monica also started to smell flowers in her car. It was the kind of smell that reminds you of a cemetery.

When they got to the home of Carol's parents, Carol asked Monica to wait while she went inside to get some money. Monica waited 15 minutes. Then she went to the door and knocked three times. A man about 50 years old, wearing pajamas, answered the door. Monica said, "I'm waiting for Carol, your daughter." The man's eyes filled with tears. "Is this a bad joke?" he said. "I did have a daughter named Carol, but her funeral was at Primavera Cemetery ten years ago today. She died in a taxi accident."

Challenge

Jan Harold Brunvand is a professor at the University of Utah in the United States. He has been collecting urban legends for years. Below are seven stories that Dr. Brunvand has determined are urban legends—that is, they are stories that many people believe are true, but are not true. There is also one story that *is* true.

Read the eight stories. Which seven stories do you think are urban legends? Which story do you think is true? (The answer is in the Answer Key.)

1. An old woman drove her car—a Mercedes—into a crowded parking lot. She drove around for a while, looking for a parking space, and finally found one. Just as she was about to pull into the space, a young man in a shiny red sports car sped around the woman and pulled into the space. He got out of his car and smiled at the woman. "Sorry," he said. "But that's what you can do when you're young and fast."

   The old woman pushed the accelerator of her Mercedes to the floor and crashed into the sports car. Then she put her car in reverse, backed up, and crashed into it again. The young man rushed over to the old woman. "What are you doing?" he yelled. The old woman handed him her insurance card and smiled. "That's what you can do when you're old and rich," she said.

2. During World War II, a German woman wrote a letter to relatives in the United States. In her letter, the woman said that she was fine. She suggested that her American cousin, Johnny, steam the stamp off the envelope to add to his stamp collection.

   The woman's relatives were puzzled. There was no Johnny in the family, nor were there any stamp collectors. The relatives realized that this was a clue. They steamed the stamp off the envelope and found that under the stamp the German woman had written in tiny letters: "Help us. We are starving."

3. Two pilots were flying an airplane with 150 passengers. The copilot left the cockpit to use the lavatory and didn't return. A long time passed. Concerned, the pilot decided to check on the copilot himself. He put the plane on autopilot and stepped out of the cockpit. Just then, the plane hit a pocket of turbulence, and the door to the cockpit slammed shut and locked. In order to get back into the cockpit, the two pilots had to smash the door with an ax in front of the terrified passengers.

4. A woman bought her boyfriend a small cellular phone. She wrapped the gift and put it on a table. The next day, all that remained of the present was torn wrapping paper. The woman searched her apartment for the phone, but found nothing. She decided to dial the phone's number and heard it ringing where her dog was sleeping. At first she thought the dog was lying on the phone, but then realized that the phone was ringing *inside* the dog. She rushed the dog to the vet, who determined that the dog had indeed swallowed the phone. The vet told the woman that her dog was in no danger and told her to let nature take its course. The phone emerged from the dog the next day in perfect working order.

5. A woman was shopping at a large department store. She put her purse down for a minute, and it was stolen.

   A few hours later, the woman was back home when the phone rang. It was a man who said he was the department store manager. He told the woman her purse was found in the store and that she could pick it up at his office.

   When the woman arrived at the store, her purse was not there, and the manager knew nothing about the phone call. The woman raced home and found her keys in the lock of her front door. When she went inside her house, she discovered that everything of value was gone.

---

6. A young woman who lived alone had a large dog—a Doberman—for protection. One day the woman came home from work and found the Doberman choking. The woman brought her dog to the vet.

   The vet examined the dog briefly and then told the woman to go back home. The vet wanted to keep the dog for a few tests and would call the woman later.

   When the woman returned home, the phone was ringing. It was the vet. "Get out of your apartment immediately!" the vet said. "Go to a neighbor's and call the police!"

   The vet had found two human fingers in the Doberman's throat. When the police arrived at the woman's apartment, they found an unconscious man in a closet. The man was bleeding and missing two fingers.

---

7. A man ate some chocolate chip cookies at a small shop in a shopping mall. He liked the cookies so much, he phoned the company the next day and asked for the recipe. A company representative told the man he could not have the recipe; it was a secret. "Well," the man asked, "would you let me buy the recipe?" The representative said he could. "How much?" the man asked. "Nine fifty," was the reply. "Just put the charge on my credit card," the man said.

   When the man received his credit card statement, he found out that he had paid nine hundred fifty dollars for the chocolate chip cookie recipe. The man tried to get his money back, but he couldn't, so he decided he was going to have nine hundred fifty dollars worth of fun. He E-mailed the recipe to everyone he knew and asked them to pass it on to someone else. Now almost everyone in the country has the "secret" recipe.

---

8. A businessman was riding the New York subway home from work. The man standing next to him kept bumping into him. The businessman became suspicious and patted his back pocket. His wallet was missing! The businessman grabbed the man and shook him. "Give me the wallet!" he demanded. The man handed him a wallet.

   When the businessman returned home that evening, he found his wallet on the dresser in his bedroom. The wallet in his pocket belonged to the man on the subway.

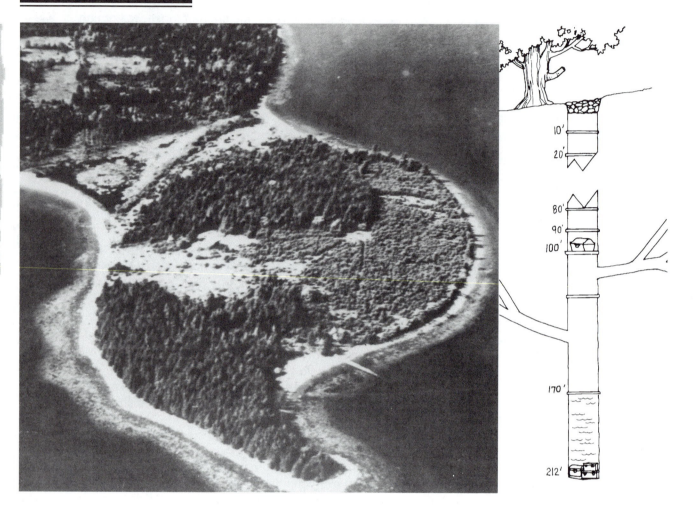

1. PRE-READING

Look at the pictures and answer the questions. Discuss your answers with your classmates.

- The small island in the picture is off the coast of eastern Canada. There is a deep hole on the island. Men began digging in the hole in 1795—and men are still digging today. What do you think they are trying to find?
- Digging in the hole is difficult. It is also dangerous: six men have died in the hole. Look at the drawing of the hole. Can you see why digging in the hole is difficult? Can you see why it is dangerous?

The Treasure Hunt

On a summer afternoon in 1795 a teenage boy named Daniel McGinnis was exploring a tiny island off the eastern coast of Canada. He was walking through a meadow of tall grass when he noticed something strange. In the center of the meadow stood a huge oak tree with part of one branch cut off. The ground beneath that branch was lower than the surrounding ground. Daniel knew that pirates had once sailed in the waters around the island. Was this, he wondered, where they had buried their treasure?

The next day Daniel returned to the island with shovels and two friends. The boys began digging. Two feet down they discovered a layer of stones. Under the stones was a hole about 13 feet wide. It was filled with loose dirt. The boys kept digging for several days. Ten feet below the ground their shovels hit an oak floor. They broke through the floor and kept digging. Twenty feet below the ground they found another oak floor. They broke through it, too, and kept digging. But when they discovered another oak floor 30 feet below the ground, they decided that they couldn't dig any deeper. They gave up the search and left the island.

Eight years later Daniel McGinnis, now a young man, returned with a group of men to continue digging beneath the oak tree. Day after day the men dug in the hole. One evening, 98 feet below the ground, their shovels hit a large wooden box. The box had to be a treasure chest! Certain that the treasure was almost theirs, the men went home to rest until daylight. When they returned in the morning, there was an unpleasant surprise: the hole had nearly filled with water. The men couldn't remove the water. Once again, Daniel McGinnis had to give up the search.

Over the years, other search groups came to the island. They all had the same problem: the hole filled with water. Not until 1850 did someone discover why.

In 1850 a man from a search group was eating his lunch on a beach not far from the hole. The man noticed water bubbling up through the sand. He went and got other men from the search group. When they saw the water coming up through the sand, they, too, thought it was odd. The men decided to dig on the beach. What they found amazed them. Under the sand there were entrances to five tunnels. All five tunnels led to the hole.

Later search groups discovered more tunnels leading from another beach to the hole. Engineers examined the tunnels. They estimated that 20 people worked two years to build them. The tunnels were cleverly planned. If anyone digging in the hole dug deeper than 95 feet, ocean water came through the tunnels and filled the hole.

Although the water problem made digging almost impossible, more and more men came to dig on the island. The tunnels convinced them that the hole held a great treasure. None of the men found the treasure, however, and six men died trying.

In 1967 a group of investors put their money into a search for the treasure. They brought huge drills, pumps, and other machines to the island. After drilling 212 feet into the hole, workers sent down a video camera. The camera took pictures of three wooden chests and a human hand. But then the walls of the hole collapsed, nearly killing a worker who was in it. The investors decided that the search was too dangerous and gave it up. Then, in 1989, they decided to try again. They raised 10 million dollars for another search. They said that this time they would not stop digging until they found the treasure.

But is there a pirates' treasure at the bottom of the hole? A lot of people think so. A brown, stringy material covered the oak floors that search groups found every ten feet in the hole. That brown material came from coconut trees. Coconut trees do not grow in Canada; the nearest coconut trees are over 800 miles away. Pirate ships could have brought the coconuts to Canada. Also, a heart-shaped stone was found in the hole. It is very similar to one that was found with pirates' treasure in the Caribbean.

If there is a pirates' treasure, it won't be easy to find. There is still the problem of water filling the hole. And there is another problem. During the past 200 years, dozens of search groups have dug in the hole, and each search group made the hole bigger. The hole that was once 13 feet wide is now enormous. The oak tree is gone. Where is the hole that Daniel McGinnis found? Today nobody knows for sure, so it is impossible to know exactly where to dig.

The investors who paid 10 million dollars think they will find the treasure in spite of the problems. And they think that when they find it, they will get every penny of their money back, and much more. One investor says, "This could be one of the greatest treasures ever found." It could be. Or it could be a 10-million-dollar hole.

2. VOCABULARY

LOOKING AT THE STORY

Write the correct word on the line.

investors	meadow	shovel	convinced
pirates	drills	chest	treasure
examining	surrounding	enormous	raised

1. Daniel was walking through the tall grass of a _____ when he noticed something strange.

2. The ground under the oak tree was different from the ground around it: it was lower than the _____ ground.

3. Robbers once sailed in ships near the coast of Canada, taking gold, silver, and jewels from other ships. Daniel wondered if perhaps the _____ had buried their _____ on the island.

4. Daniel wanted to dig under the oak tree, so he returned to the island with two friends and a _____.

5. When Daniel returned to the island to dig eight years later, his shovel hit a large wooden box. Was the box filled with gold and silver? Was the box a treasure _____?

6. Engineers looked at the tunnels very carefully. After _____ them, the engineers estimated that 20 people had built them.

7. When the men discovered the tunnels, they were sure that someone had buried something very important in the hole. The tunnels _____ them that the hole held a great treasure.

8. In 1967, men brought machines to the island to help them dig. The huge _____ dug a hole 212 feet deep.

9. Some people have put their money into a search for the treasure. These _____ think they will get every penny of their money back, and much more.

10. In 1989, the investors collected a lot of money to look for the treasure. They _____ 10 million dollars for another search.

11. Each search group has made the hole bigger. The hole that was once 13 feet wide is now _____.

LOOKING AT SPECIAL EXPRESSIONS

Find the best way to complete each sentence. Write the letter of your answer on the line.

to give up = to stop working at; to stop trying

1. The boys decided that they couldn't dig any deeper and _____

2. I used to run a mile a day, _____

3. He tried to call his mother yesterday, but the line was busy; _____

a. but I hurt my leg and had to give up running.

b. gave up their search.

c. he dialed her number for twenty minutes and then gave up.

3. COMPREHENSION/READING SKILLS

UNDERSTANDING TIME RELATIONSHIPS

What information is *not* correct? Draw a line through it.

1. Before 1795
   a. a deep hole was dug on an island.
   b. tunnels were built from beaches to the hole.
   c. ~~the walls of the hole collapsed.~~
   d. pirates sailed in the waters off the eastern coast of Canada.

2. In 1795
   a. Daniel McGinnis discovered an oak tree with part of one branch cut off.
   b. Daniel McGinnis and two friends dug under the oak tree.
   c. investors raised lots of money to search for the treasure.
   d. oak floors were found, ten, twenty, and thirty feet below the ground.

3. Eight years after Daniel McGinnis discovered the hole,
   a. he returned with a group of men to continue digging.
   b. men digging 98 feet down hit a wooden object with their shovels.
   c. the hole filled with water.
   d. six men died trying to find the treasure.

4. In 1850
   a. a man from a search group ate his lunch on a beach not far from the hole.
   b. investors brought huge drills, pumps, and other machines to the island.
   c. a search group saw water coming up through the sand.
   d. men found tunnels that led from a beach to the hole.

5. In 1967
   a. a group of investors decided to put their money into a search for the treasure.
   b. workers drilled 212 feet and then sent down a video camera.
   c. workers discovered a layer of stones in the hole.
   d. the walls of the hole collapsed, nearly killing a worker who was in it.

SCANNING FOR INFORMATION

The underlined information is not correct. Find the correct information in the story and write it. Work quickly; try to complete this exercise in three minutes or less.

1. In 1795 a teenage boy named Daniel <u>McDonald</u> was exploring a tiny island off the eastern coast of Canada.

2. In the center of the meadow stood a huge <u>maple</u> tree with part of one branch cut off.

3. <u>Two days later</u> Daniel returned to the island with shovels and two friends.

4. <u>Three</u> feet down they discovered a layer of stones.

5. Under the stones was a hole about <u>12</u> feet wide.

6. <u>Ten</u> years later Daniel McGinnis, now a young man, returned with a group of men to continue digging beneath the oak tree.

7. One <u>afternoon</u>, 98 feet below the ground, their shovels hit a large wooden box.

8. In <u>1860</u> a man from a search group was eating his lunch on a beach not far from the hole.

9. Under the sand the man found entrances to <u>four</u> tunnels.

10. Engineers estimate that <u>40</u> people worked two years to build them.

4. DISCUSSION

A. Talk about the hole. First answer the questions by checking (✔) "yes" or "no."

	Yes	No
1. The hole, with its oak floors and water tunnels, is complicated. Many people say that no group of pirates could have dug the hole. What do you think? Did pirates dig the hole?		
2. Do you think that there is a great treasure in the hole?		
3. If you had $10,000, would you invest your money in a search for the treasure?		
4. Would you like to go to the island and dig for the treasure?		

Now work as a class and answer these questions.

1. How many students think that pirates dug the hole? (If the pirates didn't dig the hole, then who did?)
2. How many students think there is a great treasure in the hole? What do they think the treasure is? How much do they think it's worth? (One investor says, "Billions of dollars." Is that possible?)
3. How many students would invest $10,000 in a search for the treasure?
4. How many students would like to go to the island and dig for the treasure? Why do those students want to go there? Why do some students not want to go there?

B. **Talk about other treasures. Think about these questions and discuss your answers with your classmates.**

1. Has a great treasure ever been discovered in your native country? What was the treasure? Who buried it? Who discovered it? What happened to it?
2. Do you know about any other searches for treasure? What were the searchers looking for? What did they find?

5. WRITING

One of the investors says, "This could be one of the greatest treasures ever found." What is your greatest treasure? Write about it. Here is what one student wrote.

My greatest treasure is my mother.

When I was little, I often had bad dreams. When I woke up, my mother always held me and took me into the garden for a short time. Then I could fall back to sleep again.

My mother always told me that I was not like other little girls. She told me I was special. Maybe that was true, and maybe it wasn't. But my mother believed it was true.

Sometimes I try to imagine that I am not my mother's daughter but someone else's daughter. I can't imagine it. I can't imagine having a different mother. She is my greatest treasure.

Challenge

In 1795 Daniel McGinnis began looking for treasure on Oak Island. Over 200 years later, people are still searching for the treasure. There is another treasure that people have been trying to find for a long time. It is Beale's treasure, which—if it exists—is buried in the United States, somewhere in Virginia. People have been looking for that treasure for more than 150 years.

Read the story of Beale's treasure.

Thomas Beale's Treasure

In 1817, 30 men, led by Thomas Beale, left their homes in Virginia to hunt in Colorado. One evening, while camping in a canyon, one of the men spotted gold in nearby rocks. The men immediately gave up hunting and began mining the gold. Later they discovered silver in the same area. Working almost constantly for 18 months, they accumulated a great treasure—1,000 pounds of gold and 2,000 pounds of silver. Worried that their treasure would be stolen, the men decided that Thomas Beale and ten of the men would transport it back to Virginia. Beale and the men would hide the treasure there and then return to the mine. The men gave Thomas Beale a second task: they told him to find a reliable man in Virginia, someone who would distribute the treasure to their families if they did not return from Colorado.

While he was in Virginia looking for a place to hide the treasure, Beale stayed at a small hotel owned by a man named Robert Morriss. Robert Morriss was an honest man, well liked by his neighbors. In the two months he stayed at Morriss's hotel, Beale got to know Morriss quite well. When Beale returned to the mine in Colorado, he recommended Morriss as a man who could be trusted with the secret of the treasure. The men approved Beale's choice.

Two years later, Beale returned to Virginia to hide another wagon load of gold and silver. Again, he stayed at Morriss's hotel. Before he went back to Colorado the third time, Beale gave Morriss an iron box to keep for him. He told Morriss to open the box if he did not come back within ten years.

Beale never returned. Morriss left the box untouched for over 20 years. In 1845, he decided that Beale had probably been killed, and he opened the iron box. What was in the box? There was a letter from Beale. In his letter, Beale told Morriss about the discovery of gold and silver in Colorado. He also told Morriss that in the box he would find three ciphers—information written in a secret code. The ciphers, Beale wrote, would lead Morriss to a great treasure. The first cipher revealed the location of the treasure; the second cipher described the treasure; and the third cipher listed the relatives of all 30 men. After he found the treasure, Morriss was to divide it into 31 parts. Thirty parts were for the families of the men who had mined the treasure in Colorado, and one part was for Morriss to keep.

Morriss looked at the ciphers. They consisted of rows and rows of numbers—over 500 numbers in each cipher. In his letter, Beale said that he would mail Morriss a decoding key—a paper that would tell Morriss what the numbers in the ciphers stood for. But in the 20 years that Morriss had kept the box, no key had ever arrived. Morriss knew that it was up to him to decode the ciphers.

Morriss never succeeded in decoding the ciphers, although he spent the rest of his life trying. Before he died in 1863, he told a friend, James Ward, about the treasure and gave him the ciphers. After years of work, Ward was able to decode cipher two, which described the treasure. He discovered that the code in cipher two was based on a U.S. document—the Declaration of Independence. Beale had given the first letter of each word in the Declaration of Independence a number:

```
 1     2  3   4     5  6    7    8 9
```
When in the course of human events, it becomes
```
10         11
```
necessary for. . . .

Now all Ward had to do was match the letters in the Declaration of Independence with the numbers in the cipher. This is the message that was revealed:

"I have deposited in the county of Bedford, about four miles from Buford's tavern, in a vault six feet below the ground the following articles belonging to the men whose names are given in Cipher Number Three . . . I deposited 2,921 pounds of gold and 5,100 pounds of silver. Also, jewels obtained in St. Louis in exchange for gold, valued at $13,000. The above is securely packed in iron pots with iron covers. The vault is roughly lined with stone, and the pots rest on solid stone. Cipher Number One describes the exact location of the vault."

For the next thirty years, Ward worked on ciphers one and three; in fact, he became obsessed with them. He neglected his family, his friends, and his business. Ultimately, he went broke and had to give up. Since he had no hope of decoding ciphers one and three himself, Ward decided to share them with the world. In 1894, he published a twenty-three-page booklet, *The Beale Papers.* In the booklet, Ward recounted the history of the ciphers and printed each of them. He ended the booklet with a warning to future treasure hunters: "Devote only such time as can be spared from your legitimate business to the task, and if you can spare no time, let the matter alone."

Since the publication of *The Beale Papers,* people have spent countless hours trying to decode the ciphers—especially cipher one, which tells where the treasure is buried. Despite Ward's warning, many people find that once they start working on the ciphers, it is difficult to "let the matter alone." They,

like Ward, become obsessed with finding solutions. There is even a club—The Beale Cypher Association—for people who are dedicated to decoding the ciphers. Anyone who joins the association receives the results of the members' work so far.

Experts who have examined the ciphers believe that the ciphers are real and have solutions. Because cipher two was based on a document, it seems likely that ciphers one and three are based on documents, too. Of course, these would have to be documents that were written before 1820, when Beale left the ciphers with Morriss. Lately most people are using computers to try to decode the ciphers. They are scanning old documents into computers and letting the computers give numbers to the letters in the documents. So far, even the computers have been unable to decode the ciphers.

Although the ciphers are certainly real, is the treasure real? Did Beale bury gold, silver, and jewels somewhere in Virginia, about four miles from Buford's Tavern? Of course, people have dug in the area. They found nothing. Perhaps the story is a hoax. Perhaps Thomas Beale made up the whole story and passed it on to Robert Morriss. Or perhaps Robert Morriss make up the whole story and passed it on to Robert Ward. Or perhaps Robert Ward made up the whole story and passed it on to the world.

It is not certain that Beale's treasure exists, yet people keep trying to decode the ciphers. Why do they continue to try? For one thing, the challenge of finding solutions to the puzzles is compelling. Some people simply want to accomplish something people have been trying to do for over 100 years. And there is another reason to persist: if Thomas Beale really did bury 8,000 pounds of gold and silver somewhere in Virginia, the treasure is worth over 20 million dollars today.

Now discuss these questions:

- Which search—the search for treasure on Oak Island or the search for Beale's treasure—do you think might be successful?
- If you had the time and money to search for treasure, which treasure would you try to find?

UNIT 11

1.   PRE-READING

Look at the picture and guess the answers to these questions.

- In what country was the picture taken?
- In what year was the picture taken?

Listen while your classmates tell their guesses. Then look in the Answer Key for the correct answers. Did the answers surprise you? Do you know anything about the Amish? If you do, tell the class what you know.

The Plain People

It is still dark when Elizabeth wakes up. She gets out of bed and shivers when her feet touch the cold, bare floor. The bedroom is not heated, and it is so cold that she can see her breath. She quickly puts on her long dress, black apron, and black shoes. Then she hurries downstairs to the kitchen.

The only light in the kitchen comes from kerosene lamps; Elizabeth's husband lit the lamps earlier, before he went out to milk the cows. Elizabeth puts a few pieces of wood into the stove and starts the fire. Then she begins to prepare a big breakfast for herself, her husband, and their six children. It is the beginning of a typical day for Elizabeth.

Although Elizabeth's day will be typical, her life is certainly not typical of modern life in the United States. Elizabeth belongs to a religious group known as the Amish. The Amish are often called the "Plain People" because they live and dress very simply. Their homes have no carpets on the floors, no pictures on the walls, and no soft, comfortable furniture. The men wear dark pants with white or blue shirts, and the women wear long dresses in dark colors. The women never wear makeup or jewelry.

The Amish have a saying: "The old way is the best way." Although the Amish accept some new ideas—they use new medicines, for example—their way of life has not changed much in 300 years. They do not use electricity, so Amish homes have no electric lights, no TVs, and no kitchen appliances like refrigerators. The Amish don't own telephones, either. They ride in buggies pulled by horses, and they speak German, the language that the first Amish people spoke.

The first Amish people lived in Germany and Switzerland. They were called Amish because their leader was Jacob Amman. The Amish were persecuted in Europe, so around 1700 they came to the New World. They settled in what is now the state of Pennsylvania.

Most of the Amish still live in Pennsylvania, although there are large communities in other states, too. All Amish, no matter where they live, have similar beliefs.

The Amish believe that life in the countryside is best. Almost all Amish live on farms. Amish farmers do not use modern machinery, yet their farms are successful because the Amish work hard and take good care of their land and animals. Their farms are always small. The Amish think it is wrong to have more land or more money than they need to live. A few years ago some Amish farmers discovered oil on their land. Was there a lot of oil under the ground, or just a little? The Amish farmers didn't want to know. They immediately sold their land and moved away, without telling anyone about the oil. They didn't want to be rich.

The Amish, who are Christians, believe they should follow the peaceful example of Jesus. Amish men will not fight in wars or serve in the army. They will not even wear coats with buttons, because military uniforms often have large gold or silver buttons.

The Amish will not buy insurance of any kind. When there is trouble, they help one another. If an Amish farmer gets sick, relatives and neighbors will milk his cows, plant his fields, and harvest his crops. If a barn burns down, as many as 200 men will come and build a new barn in one day.

The Amish are not allowed to marry people who are not Amish. That has caused a peculiar problem. The 500 or so Amish who came to the New World in the 1700s had about 40 last names. The 100,000 Amish who live in the United States today are the descendants of those people—and have the same 40 last names. In one school in Pennsylvania, 95 percent of the students—and their teacher—have the last name "Stolzfus." The Amish custom of choosing first names from the Bible adds to the problem. In one small Amish community there are 11 men named Daniel Miller!

To avoid confusion, the Amish give nicknames to people who have the same name. Some nicknames have an obvious explanation: "Chicken Dan" sells chickens, for example; "Curly Dan" has curly hair. But what about "Gravy Dan"? How did he get his nickname? At dinner one evening this Dan wanted to pour some cream into his coffee. He reached for the pitcher of cream but took the pitcher of gravy by mistake and poured gravy into his coffee. Ever since that evening, his nickname has been "Gravy Dan."

People are curious about the lives of Amish like Elizabeth and Gravy Dan. Every year thousands of tourists visit the part of Pennsylvania where most Amish live. They take pictures of the black buggies and the plain white houses. They watch Amish children as they walk to school and Amish men as they work in their fields. Most Amish are not happy about the tourists, but they tolerate them. Perhaps the Amish understand that the tourists want to experience, at least for a few days, the quieter, simpler Amish way of life.

2. VOCABULARY

LOOKING AT THE STORY

Which words have the same meaning as the words in the story? Circle the letter of the correct answer.

1. Elizabeth shivers when her feet touch the cold, *bare floor.*
   a. floor that is not covered with a carpet
   b. floor that is painted white

2. They do not use electricity, so Amish people have no kitchen *appliances* like refrigerators.
   a. machines run by electricity and used in the house
   b. furniture made out of wood and used in the house

3. *The Amish were persecuted* in Europe, so they came to the New World.
   a. People didn't like them and were cruel to them
   b. People liked them and were friendly to them

4. They *settled* in what is now the state of Pennsylvania.
   a. found a new leader
   b. came to live

5. There are large Amish *communities* in other states, too.
   a. groups of people who left their countries because of politics
   b. groups of people who live together

6. All Amish have similar *beliefs.*
   a. objects that are important to them
   b. ideas that they think are true

7. Amish men will not fight in wars. They will not even wear coats with buttons because *military uniforms* often have large gold or silver buttons.
   a. the clothes worn by schoolchildren
   b. the clothes worn by soldiers

8. If an Amish farmer gets sick, relatives and neighbors will *harvest his crops.*
   a. pick the fruit, vegetables, and grain that he grows
   b. bring him the medicine and other things that he needs

9. If a *barn* burns down, as many as 200 men will come and build a new barn in one day.
   a. a house that is made of wood and built by hand
   b. a building where a farmer keeps his crops and animals

10. The Amish are not allowed to marry people who are not Amish. That has caused a *peculiar* problem.
    a. big
    b. strange

11. A man took a pitcher of *gravy* by mistake and poured the gravy into his coffee.
    a. a drink made with lemons, water, and sugar
    b. a sauce for meat and potatoes

12. Most Amish are not happy about the tourists, but they *tolerate them.*
    a. allow them to come
    b. make them pay

LOOKING AT A NEW CONTEXT

Complete the sentences to show that you understand the meanings of the new words. In small groups, take turns reading your sentences aloud. Ask your classmates questions about their sentences.

1. A new kitchen appliance that my family really needs is a _____.

2. A modern-day example of people who are persecuted is _____.

3. If I had to leave my native country, I would settle in _____.

4. A strong belief I have is that _____.

5. Some crops that are harvested near my native city are _____.

6. Something I could never tolerate is _____.

3. COMPREHENSION/READING SKILLS

UNDERSTANDING THE MAIN IDEAS

What information is *not* in the story? Draw a line through the information.

1. Elizabeth
   a. sleeps in a bedroom that is not heated.
   b. wears a long dress, black apron, and black shoes.
   c. ~~has two sons.~~
   d. cooks on a wood stove.

2. The Amish
   a. are a religious group also called the "Plain People."
   b. live and dress very simply.
   c. live in California.
   d. believe that "the old way is the best way."

3. The first Amish people
   a. spoke French.
   b. were led by Jacob Amman.
   c. were persecuted in Europe.
   d. came to the New World around 1700.

4. Some Amish beliefs are:
   a. Life in the countryside is best.
   b. Follow the peaceful example of Jesus.
   c. Do not buy insurance.
   d. Do not work on Mondays.

UNDERSTANDING SUPPORTING DETAILS

Find the best way to complete each sentence. Write the letter of your answer on the line.

1. Elizabeth's life is not typical of life today in the United States. For example, _____

2. The Amish dress very simply. For example, _____

3. The Amish way of life has not changed much in 300 years. For example, _____

4. The Amish help one another when there is trouble. For example, _____

5. Some nicknames have an obvious explanation. For example, _____

a. they still speak German, the language that the first Amish people spoke.

b. "Chicken Dan" sells chickens and "Curly Dan" has curly hair.

c. she cooks on a wood stove.

d. if a barn burns down, as many as 200 men will come and build a new barn in a day.

e. the women wear long dresses in dark colors.

4. DISCUSSION

A. **Think about these questions. Discuss your answers with your classmates.**

1. The Amish have rules for living and dressing. Are there any religious groups in your native country that have special rules for living and dressing? Tell your classmates about them.

2. Could you live the way the Amish live? Could you live without electricity, without a car, and without a telephone?

3. Some Amish beliefs are: it is wrong to have more money than you need; never fight in wars; help one another when there is trouble. What do you think about these beliefs? Do you agree with them?

4. There is confusion because many Amish have the same last name. Are there some last names that many people in your native country have? What are the names?

5. The Amish give one another nicknames. Do you have a nickname? What is it? Is there a story behind your nickname, like the story of "Gravy Dan"?

B. **Write about a religion you know by answering the questions in the chart on the following page. Then ask a classmate the questions and write your classmate's answers in the chart.**

	You	Your Classmate
1. Which religion do you know the most about?		
2. Where does this religion get its name?		
3. Does this religion have many different groups? If so, what are some of them called?		
4. Is there a holy book? What is it called?		
5. Is any day of the week special? Which day? What do people do on that day?		
6. Which religious holiday is most important? What does the holiday celebrate? What do people do on that holiday?		
7. Are there any rules about food?		
8. Are there any rules about clothing?		
9. What does this religion say happens to people after they die?		

5. WRITING

Write about one of the world's religions. Use the information you wrote in Discussion Exercise 4B, or use the information your classmate gave you. Here is what one student wrote.

The Mormon religion is a Christian religion that Joseph Smith began about 150 years ago. Most Mormons live in the United States, in the state of Utah.

Mormons have a lot of rules. They don't drink alcohol. They also don't drink coffee, tea, cola, or any drink that has caffeine in it. They must pay the church 10 percent of their income.

In the Mormon church there are no paid priests or ministers. People volunteer to work as ministers.

Years ago Mormon men had more than one wife. The Mormons' neighbors and the U. S. government didn't like that, and there was a lot of trouble. But today Mormon men have just one wife.

Challenge

Read the paragraphs that give information about Amish life. Then match each paragraph with the photo that fits it best. Write the number of the paragraph below the photo. Be sure to read each paragraph to the end before you make your choice.

1. When Amish boys are 16, they are given special buggies, called courting buggies, so that they can give girls rides. Some boys add carpeting to their buggies and install stereos. This is actually against the Amish practice of being plain, but adults tolerate it. Some boys even add speedometers so they can see if their buggies can go faster than the average speed of a buggy, which is about 12 miles per hour. One Amish man said, "If you clock a buggy going 15 miles an hour, you can be sure it's a teenage driver!" It is easy to tell a courting buggy from a regular buggy. A regular buggy is covered and looks like a box sitting on wheels, but a courting buggy is open, with no roof.

2. The Amish have a saying: "The more you learn, the more you are confused." The Amish believe that education after the eighth grade—that is, after a child is thirteen or fourteen—is unnecessary. That belief caused a serious problem for the Amish in the 1960s. Some states began enforcing laws that require school attendance until age 16, and Amish teenagers had to go to high school. In some cases, police forced Amish children onto school buses while their parents stood by, crying and praying. The Amish did nothing to change the law because they believed that any type of protest—even filing a lawsuit—was wrong. Many non-Amish, however, wanted to help. They formed a group called the National Committee for Amish Religious Freedom and filed a lawsuit. The case was decided by the United States Supreme Court in 1972. The court ruled unanimously that Amish children were exempt from the law and could leave school after the eighth grade. So, today Amish children are educated in the same way their parents and grandparents were educated—by Amish teachers in one-room schoolhouses. Their formal education stops after eight years.

3. Amish families gather every other Sunday for a worship service that lasts four hours. At an Amish service, men and women sit separately on wooden benches, and the children sit on benches at the back of the room. (Halfway through the service, the children are given a snack to help them make it to the next meal.) When the service is over, the benches are removed and tables are set up for lunch. The meal is simple but plentiful: There are sandwiches and soup; pickles and pickled beets; bread, butter, and jam; and pies and cake for dessert. Amish services, as well as the meal that follows them, take place not in church buildings—the Amish have no churches—but in people's homes. Anyone on a Sunday drive through the Amish countryside can easily tell where the Sunday services are being held: There will be twenty to thirty-five buggies parked outside the house.

4. The Amish are one of the fastest-growing religious groups in the United States because Amish families have so many children. The average number of children in an Amish family is six, but families with eleven or twelve children are not uncommon. Their growing population has caused a hard-to-solve problem for the Amish. Farmland has become expensive in the United States, and most Amish cannot afford to buy it. As a result, the Amish have too little land for too many people. Some Amish have turned to professions other than farming, with furniture-making being the most popular. Amish-made furniture, which is sold in stores all over the United States, is prized for its quality and durability.

5. In 1985 the movie *Witness* was filmed in Lancaster, Pennsylvania, the home of many Amish. The movie tells the story of an Amish widow who falls in love with a police detective from Philadelphia, played by Harrison Ford. The movie was made without the permission of the Amish, who opposed the film. One scene in the movie particularly offended the Amish. Harrison Ford, dressed in plain clothes, defends his Amish friends in a fist fight. That scene was filmed in front of Zimmerman's Hardware Store, where Amish actually shop. Later, laws were passed in Pennsylvania to protect the Amish from similar movies being made without their permission.

a. _____

b. _____

c. _____

d. _____

e. _____

UNIT 12

1. PRE-READING

Think about these questions. Discuss your answers with your classmates.

- Do you know of any old person who died soon after an important event, like a holiday or birthday?
- Do you think that people can control the time of their own deaths?

Postponing Death

Yinlan looked at the people sitting around the table and smiled contentedly. Everyone in her family was there—her children, her grandchildren, and her new great-grandson, just one month old. Her whole family had come to celebrate the Harvest Moon Festival.

The Harvest Moon Festival is a Chinese celebration. Although Yinlan no longer lived in China—she lived in San Francisco—she and her family still celebrated the Harvest Moon Festival just as Yinlan had in China. At the time of the full moon in August or September, her family gathered at her house for dinner. After dinner they ate moon cakes, a special round cookie. Then, if the sky was clear, they always walked outside to admire the full moon.

Tonight there was not a cloud in the sky, and the full moon shone brightly. Yinlan suggested that they all go outside. Her grandson helped her up from her chair. As Yinlan and her grandson walked toward the door, she held on to his arm and leaned against him for support. Yinlan was 86 years old. She had not been well the past few months, and her family noticed that she seemed weak.

Two days after the Harvest Moon Festival, Yinlan died peacefully in her sleep. Her family was sad but at the same time grateful. They felt happy that they had been able to celebrate the Harvest Moon Festival with her one last time. Everyone said it was remarkable that Yinlan had died just two days after the holiday.

Actually, the timing of Yinlan's death was not remarkable at all. Recently, sociologists studied the death rate among elderly Chinese women in California. They discovered that the death rate drops 35 percent before the Harvest Moon Festival and then rises 35 percent: Each year there are fewer deaths than usual the week before the festival and more deaths than usual the week after. Sociologists believe that these changes in the death rate show the mind's power over the body. The Harvest Moon Festival, when families gather, is important to elderly Chinese women. Apparently some women are able to postpone their deaths so that they can celebrate the festival one last time.

Sociologists also studied the death rate of elderly Jewish men around the time of Passover, a Jewish holiday. They discovered the same phenomenon. During the week before Passover, the death rate among elderly Jewish men drops 24 percent. The week after Passover, the death rate rises 24 percent. It seems that Jewish men, like Chinese women, wait until after the holiday to die. Why?

Passover is a Jewish religious holiday that is a family holiday as well. On the first two days of Passover, families gather in their homes for a ceremony. They sit around a table to share a special meal and to listen to the story of Passover. Traditionally, the oldest man in the family sits at the head of the table and reads the story. It is an important event for elderly Jewish men—so important that some men postpone their deaths until after Passover.

The idea that people can postpone the time of their deaths is not new. Many families tell stories of a relative who held on to life until after an important event. They tell of a grandmother who died after the birth of a grandchild, a grandfather who died after his 92nd birthday party. The stories people tell, however, are just that: stories. They are not proof that people can postpone their deaths. The sociologists' work is important because the sociologists studied facts, not stories. The facts— the drop and rise in death rates—prove that people really can postpone their deaths.

One famous person who may have postponed his death was Thomas Jefferson. Thomas Jefferson wrote the Declaration of Independence, one of the most important U.S. documents. The Declaration of Independence was signed on July 4, 1776. Thomas Jefferson died exactly fifty years later, on July 4, 1826. He died after asking his doctor, "Is it the Fourth?"

Historians have always thought that Jefferson's death on the Fourth of July was a remarkable coincidence. It now seems quite possible that the timing of Jefferson's death was no coincidence at all.

2. VOCABULARY

LOOKING AT THE STORY

Which words have the same meaning as the words in the story? Circle the letter of your answer.

1. Yinlan looked at the people sitting around the table and smiled *contentedly*.
   - **a.** nervously
   - **b.** happily

2. Yinlan's family celebrated the Harvest Moon Festival *just* as Yinlan had in China.
   - **a.** exactly
   - **b.** almost

3. Her family *gathered* at her house for dinner.
   - **a.** came together
   - **b.** cooked

4. Her family was sad, but at the same time *grateful*.
   - **a.** not surprised
   - **b.** thankful

5. It was *remarkable* that Yinlan had died just two days after the holiday.
   - **a.** unusual; surprising
   - **b.** sad; depressing

6. Sociologists studied *the death rate* among elderly Chinese women in California.
   - **a.** the number of deaths compared to the number of people
   - **b.** the number of people who die in a foreign country

7. The death rate *drops* 35 percent before the Harvest Moon Festival.
   - **a.** goes up
   - **b.** goes down

8. The death rate *rises* 35 percent after the festival.
   - **a.** goes up
   - **b.** goes down

9. *Apparently* some women are able to postpone their deaths.
   - **a.** It seems that
   - **b.** It is lucky that

10. Sociologists who studied the death rate of elderly Jewish men around the time of Passover discovered the same *phenomenon*.
    - **a.** fact or event that is unusual and interesting
    - **b.** holiday that is celebrated by families

11. Some Jewish men *postpone their deaths until after Passover*.
    - **a.** wait until after Passover to die
    - **b.** hope that they will not die until after Passover

12. The Declaration of Independence is one of the most important U.S. *documents*.
    - **a.** buildings
    - **b.** papers

13. Historians thought that Jefferson's death on the Fourth of July was a *coincidence*.
    - **a.** an event that makes people feel sad
    - **b.** two events that accidentally happen at the same time

LOOKING AT SPECIAL EXPRESSIONS

Find the best way to complete each sentence. Write the letter of your answer on the line.

to grow up = to change from a child to a man or woman

1. Yinlan now lives in the United States, but ____

2. When the little girl grows up, ____

3. Because he grew up on a farm, ____

a. he knows how to take care of animals.

b. she wants to be a doctor.

c. she grew up in China.

3. COMPREHENSION/READING SKILLS

UNDERSTANDING THE MAIN IDEAS

What information is not in the story? Draw a line through the information.

1. Yinlan
   a. celebrated the Harvest Moon Festival with her family.
   b. was 86 years old.
   c. died two days after the Harvest Moon Festival.
   d. ~~lived in a small apartment in San Francisco.~~

2. Sociologists
   a. studied the death rate among elderly Chinese women in San Francisco.
   b. believe that Chinese women live long because they eat a healthy diet.
   c. discovered that there are fewer deaths before the Harvest Moon Festival and more deaths after it.
   d. believe that the changes in the death rate show the mind's power over the body.

3. What happens during Passover?
   a. Families gather in their homes for a ceremony.
   b. Families share a special meal.
   c. Children eat moon-shaped cookies.
   d. The oldest man in the family reads the story of Passover.

4. Sociologists
   a. studied the death rate of elderly Jewish men around the time of Passover.
   b. discovered that their death rate drops 24 percent before Passover.
   c. discovered that their death rate rises 24 percent after Passover.
   d. went to Jewish homes to learn how Jews celebrate Passover.

5. The sociologists' work on death rates
   a. is important.
   b. was a study of facts, not stories.
   c. was done in 1996.
   d. proves that people really can postpone their deaths.

6. Thomas Jefferson
   a. wrote the Declaration of Independence.
   b. was the second president of the United States.
   c. died on July 4, 1826—exactly fifty years after the Declaration of Independence was signed.
   d. may have postponed his death.

SCANNING FOR INFORMATION

The underlined information is not correct. Find the correct information in the story and write it. Work quickly; try to complete the exercise in three minutes or less.

1. Yinlan died <u>five</u> days after the Harvest Moon Festival.

2. Recently, sociologists studied the death rate among elderly Chinese women in <u>Florida</u>.

3. They discovered that the death rate drops <u>24</u> percent before the Harvest Moon Festival.

4. Sociologists also studied the death rate of elderly Jewish men at the time of <u>Hanukkah</u>, a Jewish holiday.

5. During the week before Passover, the death rate drops <u>23</u> percent.

6. On the first <u>three</u> days of Passover, families gather in their homes for a ceremony.

7. One famous person who may have postponed his death was <u>William</u> Jefferson.

8. Jefferson was the author of the <u>Bill of Rights</u>, one of the most important U.S. documents.

9. The Declaration of Independence was signed on July 4, <u>1774</u>.

10. Jefferson died exactly <u>40</u> years later.

4. DISCUSSION

Think about these questions. Discuss your answers with your classmates.

1. One question in the prereading exercise was: "Do you think people can control the time of their own deaths?" After reading the story, is your answer to that question still the same, or has it changed?
2. After reading "Postponing Death," do you now think someone you know may have postponed his or her death? Tell your classmates about it.
3. Do you think the mind has power over the body? Do you think, for example, that people can control whether or not they get sick or feel pain?
4. The Harvest Moon Festival is important to the Chinese, and Passover is important to Jews. Is there a holiday that is important to you—so important that you would postpone your death to experience it one last time?
5. Thomas Jefferson died on July 4, 1826—50 years after the Declaration of Independence was signed. That was a remarkable coincidence. Do you know of a remarkable coincidence? Tell your classmates about it.

5. WRITING

A. The sociologists believe that their studies show the mind's power over the body. Have you ever used your mind to control your body? Do you know a story that shows that the mind can control the body? Write a paragraph or two. Here is what one student wrote.

I read a story in the newspaper about an elderly woman who was dying in a hospital. She asked the doctor to call her only son because she wanted to see him one last time. But before her son arrived, the woman's heart stopped beating. The doctor met the woman's son in the lobby of the hospital and told him that his mother had died. When the son went to his mother's room and began to cry, a machine connected to the woman showed that the woman's heart was beating again. The woman opened her eyes, looked at her son, and smiled. A few minutes later she peacefully left the world again.

B. Write about a holiday that is important to you. How do you celebrate it? Here is what one student wrote.

When I was a little girl, my favorite day was March 3. That is when people in Japan celebrate Hinamatsuri, a holiday for girls. The girls dress dolls in beautiful dresses called kimonos and display the dolls. Girls usually get the dolls ready about a week before the holiday. (People say that girls who dress their dolls early get married early, but that wasn't true for me! I always dressed my dolls early, but I am twenty-six years old and not married.) The first time a girl celebrates Hinamatsuri, her relatives come to her house. Everybody drinks "Shirozake," a special drink, and eats sweets we call "Sakuramochi." The next day, on March 4, the girls put their dolls away. I always felt a little sad when Hinamatsuri was over and it was time to put my dolls away.

Challenge

PART 1

Below you will read about guided imagery. Dr. David Bresler, director of the Academy for Guided Imagery in California, says, "Many people practice guided imagery without realizing it. Worrying is a good example. People who worry a lot are good at using imagery." How is worrying similar to guided imagery? How is it different? Read the information below. Then write your answer in a paragraph.

Mind Over Matter?

The death rate of elderly Chinese women falls 35 percent before the Harvest Moon Festival and rises 35 percent after it. These statistics indicate that people can control the timing of their deaths. If that is so, then there is apparently a connection between the mind and the body. If you'd like to experience the mind-body connection yourself, do this simple experiment.

Imagine that you are standing in the kitchen. Take a few minutes to look around the kitchen that you see in your mind. Notice the color of the kitchen table, appliances, and cupboards. Notice, too, any kitchen sounds, like the hum of the refrigerator. Notice any smells. Now imagine that a cutting board is in front of you. Next to it is a sharp knife.

Next, imagine that on the cutting board there is a fresh, juicy lemon. In your mind, hold the lemon in one hand. Feel its weight and texture. Then put it back on the board. Carefully cut it in half with the knife. Feel the resistance to the knife. Now look at the two halves of the lemon. Notice the yellow pulp and the white inner peel. See whether you have cut through a seed or two. Carefully cut one of the two halves in two. See where a drop or two of lemon juice has collected on the surface of one of the quarters. Imagine lifting this lemon wedge to your mouth. Smell the sharp, fresh scent. Now bite into the sour, juicy lemon.

Is your mouth watering? If you're like most people, it is.

You have just experienced guided imagery. Guided imagery uses the power of the mind to cause physical changes in the body. You see, hear, feel, and taste things in your imagination, and your body reacts to the images. (It is called "guided" because usually someone else tells you what to imagine.) Champion athletes having been using guided imagery for years.

Before they compete, they repeatedly visualize themselves performing calmly and perfectly. The benefits of guided imagery are so accepted in the world of sports that three out of four Olympic athletes now practice some form of guided imagery.

More recently, doctors have begun using guided imagery with their patients, sometimes with astounding results. Doctors at the Cleveland Clinic in the United States wanted to test the effects of guided imagery on patients who were going to have surgery. So they did an experiment. They divided 130 patients into two groups. One group received standard care, while the other group listened to guided imagery tapes for three days before and six days after surgery. With a background of soothing music, the tapes instructed patients to imagine that they were in calm, beautiful surroundings with someone they loved beside them. Then they were encouraged to imagine themselves in the operating room, having the surgery with little pain or fear. On the day of the surgery, all patients were asked to rate their anxiety level on a scale from 0 to 100, with 0 meaning no anxiety and 100 meaning extreme anxiety. The control group rated their anxiety as 73; the guided imagery group rated their anxiety as 38. The guided imagery group not only felt less anxious; they apparently felt less pain. All patients had medication pumps which allowed them to give themselves painkillers as they needed them. The guided imagery group used 37 percent less pain medicine.

The doctors were especially interested in knowing how much pain medicine their patients used because that amount is an objective, measurable quantity. Like the sociologists' statistics, it is a fact that seems to demonstrate once again the mind's power over the body.

PART 2

Guided imagery sessions usually begin this way: First, you find a comfortable position, lying down or in a comfortable chair, and you close your eyes. Next, you are helped to relax, perhaps by breathing deeply or by relaxing each part of your body, from your head to your toes. Then you are guided to imagery that is just for you. For example, a tennis player is guided into visualizing a perfect game, and a patient is guided into visualizing successful surgery.

Following are two guided imagery scripts. Read each script. Who do you think each script is for? Here are some possibilities:

People who . . .
   a. are going to have surgery
   b. have trouble sleeping
   c. want to lose weight
   d. have allergies

Write the letter of your answer on the line.

1. ____ Imagine a softness all around you . . . a generous cushion of warmth and protection . . . a gentle sense of safety surrounding you . . . as you continue to breathe deeply . . .

And perhaps even imagining that this cushion of energy is drawing to it all the love and sweetness that anyone has ever felt for you at any time . . . pulling in all the caring and loving kindness that has ever been sent your way . . . every prayer and good wish . . . pulling it all in like a powerful magnet . . .

And perhaps even sensing the presence of all those who have loved you well in the past . . . those who care for you . . . either real or imaginary . . . perhaps even seeing a special face . . . hearing a kind, familiar voice . . . feeling a loving touch . . .

Allowing yourself to surrender into this feeling of comfort and safety . . . like a dearly loved child, valued and protected, tucked in for the night . . . surrounded by soft quilts and sweet dreams . . . perfectly, utterly safe . . .

And so you are . . .

2. ____ Imagine that from somewhere above you . . . a cone of powerful white light is softly and steadily moving down . . . surrounding and protecting you . . . keeping out anything that might harm or irritate you . . . so you can be safe and comfortable . . .

Feeling the light soak into places that are swollen and sore . . . and sensing them begin to shrink back to normal size . . . perhaps opening passageways for breathing . . . gently warming and widening the airways in the head, neck, and chest . . . making even more room for the gentle flow of sweet, vital air . . . making it easy to breathe . . .

And see the light . . . like a flare . . . highlighting and magnifying the cells that are accustomed to reacting quickly to irritation . . . and sending them a clear, calming message to settle down . . . and save their energy for the real enemies of the body . . . not these neutral particles that mean no harm . . .

And so . . . feeling relaxed and safe and comfortable . . . you watch as the light slowly begins to withdraw to wherever it came from . . . until it is gone altogether for now . . . knowing it is yours to call forth again . . . whenever you wish . . .

UNIT 13

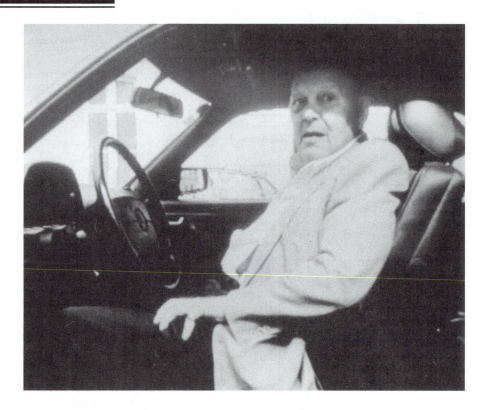

1. PRE-READING

Imagine that after shopping, you return to your car, which is parked in a parking lot. It is nine o'clock at night, and there are only a few people in the parking lot. When you get into your car, a man jumps up from the backseat, holds a gun to your head, and says, "Drive!" What would you do? Check an answer, or write your own answer. Then compare your answer with those of your classmates.

I would . . .

1. _____ scream and yell to get the attention of the people in the parking lot.

2. _____ try to grab the gun.

3. _____ tell the man I'll drive him where he wants to go, but then drive to a police station.

4. _____ drive where the man tells me to go.

5. _____ _____

An Unexpected Adventure

One summer afternoon Jean and Clothilde Lestarquit, an elderly couple, visited their daughter at her home in Lille, France. A few minutes before six o'clock, the Lestarquits decided to leave. They said good-bye to their daughter, walked to their car, and got in. They expected a quiet, uneventful ride home. The ride, however, was anything but quiet and uneventful.

Mr. Lestarquit was about to start the car when a gunman jumped up from the backseat. He held a gun to Mr. Lestarquit's head. "Drive me to Paris!" he demanded.

"All right," Mr. Lestarquit replied. "I'll drive you anywhere you want to go. But first let my wife out of the car."

The gunman agreed to let Mrs. Lestarquit go. After she was safely out of the car, Mr. Lestarquit started the engine, pulled away from the curb, and drove down the street. He was driving slowly, but his mind was racing. Unarmed and 81 years old, he knew he could not fight the gunman. He knew he needed help. Where were the police? As he drove through each intersection, he looked up and down the side streets, hoping to spot a police car. There was none in sight. "Just my luck," he thought. "If I were speeding, there would be a police car on every corner."

Suddenly Mr. Lestarquit realized how he could attract the attention of the police. He pushed his foot down on the accelerator of his Mercedes, and the car sped forward. "What are you doing?" shouted the gunman. "Avoiding the police," Mr. Lestarquit lied. "I thought I saw a police car back there."

Mr. Lestarquit began driving like a madman. He drove 60 miles an hour on side streets, ran red lights, and drove the wrong way on one-way streets. On two-way streets he drove on the wrong side of the road. Not one police officer saw him.

Obviously, Mr. Lestarquit's plan was not working. He needed a new plan. But what? Suddenly he remembered that the Lille police station was only a few blocks away. "All right," he thought. "If I can't bring the police to my car, I'll bring my car to the police."

He turned a corner and saw the police station ahead. Immediately his heart sank. There was a courtyard in front of the police station, and the two large doors that led to the courtyard were closed. Mr. Lestarquit hesitated for a moment. Then he pushed the accelerator to the floor and steered straight for the doors.

The car crashed through the doors and stopped in the courtyard. Mr. Lestarquit yelled, "Help! He's going to kill me!" Then he reached back to grab the man's gun. Just as he grabbed it, the gunman pulled the trigger. The bullet grazed Mr. Lestarquit's hand and went through the windshield. Before the gunman could pull the trigger again, Mr. Lestarquit opened the car door and fell to the ground. Officers from the police station, who had come running when they heard the crash, quickly captured the gunman. It was 6:30 P.M.—exactly 35 minutes since the Lestarquits had left their daughter's house on a quiet street in Lille.

It seemed to Jean Lestarquit that for those 35 minutes he had stepped out of reality and into an action movie. There were so many things action movies have—a gunman, a hero, a speeding car, and a car crash. Fortunately for Jean Lestarquit, there was one more thing most action movies have: a happy ending.

2. VOCABULARY

LOOKING AT THE STORY

Write the correct word on the line.

grazed	windshield	elderly	courtyard	demanded	ran
accelerator	captured	spot	unarmed	hesitated	sped

1. Mr. Lestarquit was 81 years old. He was not young; he was _____.

2. When the gunman spoke to Mr. Lestarquit, he was not polite. "Take me to Paris!" he _____.

3. Mr. Lestarquit did not have a gun. He was _____.

4. Mr. Lestarquit looked for a police car, but there was none in sight. He couldn't _____ one anywhere.

5. Mr. Lestarquit wanted to go fast, so he put his foot down on the _____.

6. Mr. Lestarquit was driving very fast; his car _____ through the streets.

7. Mr. Lestarquit didn't stop at red lights; he _____ the red lights.

8. The building in the picture has a _____.

9. When Mr. Lestarquit saw that the doors to the courtyard were closed, he stopped to think. He _____ for a moment.

10. The bullet touched the skin on Mr. Lestarquit's hand as it went past. Mr. Lestarquit was not badly hurt because the bullet only _____ his hand.

11. When the bullet went out the front of the car, it broke the glass in the _____.

12. It took only a few minutes for the police to take the gunman and bring him to the police station. The police _____ the gunman quickly.

LOOKING AT SPECIAL EXPRESSIONS

Find the best way to complete each sentence. Write the letter of your answer on the line.

anything but = not at all

1. The ride, however, _____

2. That bridge _____

3. That restaurant _____

a. is anything but safe.

b. is anything but inexpensive.

c. was anything but quiet and uneventful.

about to = to be ready to

4. Mr. Lestarquit was about to start the car _____

5. We were about to play tennis _____

6. I was about to buy a jacket for $60 _____

d. when a gunman jumped up from the floor of the backseat.

e. when I saw a nicer one for $50.

f. when it started to rain.

3. COMPREHENSION/READING SKILLS

UNDERSTANDING TIME RELATIONSHIPS

What information is *not* correct? Draw a line through it.

1. About six o'clock Mr. and Mrs. Lestarquit
   a. decided to leave their daughter's house.
   b. ~~arrived home safely.~~
   c. said good-bye to their daughter.
   d. walked to their car and got in.

2. Mr. Lestarquit was about to start the car when a gunman
   a. jumped up from the backseat.
   b. held a gun to Mr. Lestarquit's head.
   c. demanded that Mr. Lestarquit drive him to Paris.
   d. pulled the trigger.

3. After Mrs. Lestarquit was out of the car, Mr. Lestarquit
   a. started the engine.
   b. pulled away from the curb.
   c. got into his car.
   d. tried to spot a police car.

4. After Mr. Lestarquit realized how he could attract the attention of the police, he

   a. drove 60 miles an hour on side streets.

   b. ran red lights.

   c. drove the wrong way on one-way streets.

   d. said, "Let my wife out of the car."

5. After Mr. Lestarquit crashed through the doors leading to the courtyard,

   a. the car stopped.

   b. he grabbed the gun.

   c. the gunman pulled the trigger.

   d. the gunman shouted, "What are you doing?"

UNDERSTANDING DETAILS

Read the sentences from the story. One word in each sentence is not correct. Find the word and cross it out. Write the correct word.

1. Jean and Clothilde Lestarquit, an elderly couple, visited their daughter at her home in Lille, Spain.

2. They said good-bye to their daughter and walked to their bicycles.

3. Mr. Lestarquit was about to start the car when a policeman jumped up from the backseat.

4. "Drive me to Barcelona!" the man demanded.

5. Mr. Lestarquit said, "I'll drive you anywhere you want to go, but first let my daughter out of the car."

Now copy three sentences from the story, but change one word in each sentence so that the information is not correct. Give your sentences to a classmate. Your classmate will find the incorrect word in each sentence, cross it out, and write the correct word. When your classmate is finished, check the corrections.

6. _____

   _____

7. _____

   _____

8. _____

   _____

4. DISCUSSION

A. Think about these questions. Discuss your answers with your classmates.

1. Do you think Mr. Lestarquit was brave or foolish? Why?
2. What would you have done if you had been in his place?

B. With a partner or in small groups, talk about what you would do in the following dangerous situations.

1. You are walking down the street when suddenly a big dog runs toward you. The dog is barking.
2. You are walking down a busy street in a big city. A man walks up to you and says, "Give me your money!" He has a knife.
3. It is 11 o'clock at night. You are home alone watching TV. There is a knock at the door. You aren't expecting anyone.
4. You come home late at night. The door to your house or apartment is open. You are sure you locked the door when you left the house. You live alone.
5. You and a friend go to a party in your friend's car. Your friend drinks beer at the party. When it is time to go home, you realize that your friend has had too much to drink.

5. WRITING

A. Write a police report. Imagine that you were one of the police officers at the Lille police station. After capturing the gunman, you asked Mr. Lestarquit what happened and then wrote down what he told you. What is your report?

B. Have you ever had an experience like Jean Lestarquit's? Have you ever been in a dangerous situation where you had to decide what to do? Write about your experience. Here is what one student wrote.

> When I was in high school I was in a dangerous situation almost every day.
>
> One day after school, a group of boys surrounded my friends and me. There were about 20 of them. There were three of us. My friends and I had to decide whether to fight or run. We decided to fight. We started to fight, and then fortunately some university students came along and separated us.
>
> There were other dangerous situations, too, but that is one I remember very well.

Challenge

Read the following stories about men who, like Mr. Lestarquit, had unexpected adventures. Would you do what Charles Gardner did? What Mark Thomas did? What Mr. Lestarquit did?

His Pride and Joy

It was not a new car—it was a 1988 model—but the car was new to Charles Gardner, and it was his pride and joy. It was a black and gray Chevrolet Suburban—a large, boxy station wagon. Charles had bought it two months ago from a used car dealer in Chicago. How Charles loved that car!

So, when Charles came out of a friend's house and saw two teenaged boys standing near his car, he was concerned. Were the boys thinking about stealing his beloved Chevy? Then Charles realized that the car's engine was running. They *were* going to steal his car! They had already started the engine!

When the boys saw Charles, they jumped into the Chevy and pulled away. Charles ran after the car and jumped on its roof. With his right hand, Charles hung on to the luggage rack on the top of the car. With his left hand, he reached into the window and grabbed the driver's neck, yelling at him to stop.

The driver wasn't about to stop. He and his buddy wanted the Chevy. They had the car. Now all they needed to do was to get its owner off the roof.

The driver saw a steel light post ahead, and he aimed for it. If he crashed into the light post, surely the man on the roof would fall off, and the car would be his. He hit the light post with such force that the post fell, and live electrical wires landed on Charles's right arm, giving him first degree burns. Still, Charles hung on.

When the driver realized that Charles was still on top of the car, he headed for Chicago's busiest expressway, an eight-lane highway that runs through the heart of the city. Crashing the car into the light post hadn't knocked Charles off the roof. Maybe high speeds would.

When the car turned onto the entrance ramp to the expressway, Charles lay down flat and held on tightly to the luggage rack. The driver pushed the accelerator to the floor, and the car sped down the expressway at 80 miles an hour. Each time the driver swerved around a car, the boxy Chevy rocked. Still, Charles hung on.

By this time, Charles's wild ride had attracted the attention of the police. Charles heard sirens and looked behind him. At least a dozen Chicago police cars had joined the chase, lights flashing, sirens wailing. Suddenly Charles had the feeling that this was not real life; it was a scene from a movie. This would actually be exciting, Charles thought, if only I weren't afraid of getting killed.

The driver heard the sirens, too. Now he had to get rid of not only Charles, but the police as well. He exited the expressway and headed for a neighborhood he knew like the back of his hand. Maybe here he could get the police off his trail and Charles off the roof of the car. He sped down alleys and drove on sidewalks. He crossed parking lots and cut through parks. He crashed into garbage cans and drove through fences. Still, Charles hung on.

Finally, the young thieves realized that, although they wanted the Chevy, Charles wanted it more. The driver stopped the car, and both boys jumped out and ran. The police caught them after a short chase on foot.

Charles climbed down from the roof and checked his car over. The front end was badly dented, but a good body shop could probably fix it.

Later, Charles was asked why he had risked his life for his car. He replied, "It was just a reaction, I guess. I wasn't trying to be a hero or anything. I was just trying to get my car back. I mean, it's my car."

A Wild Ride

Fourteen dollars of unleaded regular nearly cost gas station owner Mark Thomas his life.

Police say he clung to the hood of a car driven by a customer who tried to run him over after a dispute over how much gas he pumped. The wild ride lasted for six miles as the woman repeatedly sped up and slammed on the brakes, trying to dislodge him from the front of her vehicle.

It started Tuesday morning when a woman pulled into the Amoco Station on Long Beach Boulevard, the main street that runs the length of Long Beach Island.

Thomas said the woman ordered a fill-up, which came to $14. But she said she only had $5, and had only asked for that much gas. When she asked if she could pay the rest next week, Thomas said no.

She started to drive away, but he reached inside and switched off the ignition.

He was standing in front of the car trying to memorize its license plate number when she started it up again and came straight at him, police said. He jumped onto the hood to avoid being run over, he said.

"I was holding onto the windshield wiper and the radio antenna," Thomas said. "She tried to shake me off by turning on the windshield wiper. Then she turned on the windshield washer spray."

Police said the ride ended without injury when the woman drove past a police officer, who pulled her over. She was charged with robbery and aggravated assault, and was released on $15,000 bail.

While clinging to the hood at speeds he estimated at 75 to 85 miles an hour, Thomas was thinking two things.

"I was thinking, 'How am I going to get off of here?' I was also thinking I should have let her pay next week."

1. PRE-READING

The people in the picture live in the small town of Wetumka, Oklahoma. They are celebrating a festival called "Sucker Day." The dictionary defines "sucker" as "a foolish person who is easily cheated." It is not a polite word.

Who do you think the sucker is? Someone in the photo? Someone else? Read the story to find out.

Sucker Day

In August 1950, a stranger drove into the small town of Wetumka, Oklahoma. He walked into the local newspaper office and introduced himself. He said that his name was F. Morrison and that he was the publicity man for a circus—a *big* circus, with elephants, tigers, clowns, and acrobats. He had exciting news: The circus was coming to Wetumka! It would arrive in just three weeks, on August 24.

Wetumka was a town of only 2,000 people, and news traveled fast. By late that afternoon, almost everyone in town had heard about the circus. The businesspeople were especially eager to hear more. A circus would bring people to town, and people would spend money in local stores and restaurants. The businesspeople wanted more information about the circus. Did Mr. Morrison have a few minutes to talk to them?

He sure did! He'd be happy to talk to them! F. Morrison told the businesspeople that the circus would attract thousands of people, so they'd better get plenty of supplies. And, he added, he wanted to tell them about a special business opportunity.

"Each person who comes to the circus will get a program," he said, "and in those programs, there will be advertisements. I can sell you advertising space right now." The cautious businesspeople of Wetumka looked at F. Morrison and said nothing. "I know, I know, you want to think it over," Mr. Morrison continued. "That's understandable, because advertising space is expensive—in fact, it's *very* expensive." The businesspeople looked at one another and frowned. "But," he went on, "you'll get more for your money than just advertising space. The circus will buy all its supplies from the businesses that advertise in the program."

"Let me give you an example. A circus sells hot dogs, right? Well, where is the circus going to buy those hot dogs? From the store that advertises in the program! Balloons? Soft drinks? Hay for the elephants? We'll buy them all from the businesses that advertise in the program. And when the circus people get hungry, where will they eat? That's right! At the restaurants that advertise in the program!"

Mr. Morrison told the businesspeople they didn't have to make up their minds right away. He'd be in town for the next two weeks doing publicity for the circus. They could pay him for advertising space anytime.

During the next two weeks, Mr. Morrison sold advertising space to almost every business in Wetumka. When he left town, his suitcase was filled with the money people had paid for advertising space.

On the morning of August 24, crowds of people poured into Wetumka, just as F. Morrison had predicted. By late morning, thousands of people were waiting along Main Street to watch for the circus, which was to arrive at noon.

At noon the circus was nowhere in sight.

At one o'clock the circus still hadn't come, and the businesspeople realized that they had been tricked. There was no circus! What suckers they were! F. Morrison had cheated them out of their money. But the money was the least of their worries. What were they going to do now about the thousands of people who were waiting for the circus? The crowd was getting more impatient by the minute. What if the hot, tired people became really angry?

The mayor of Wetumka made a quick and wise decision. He told the people that, unfortunately, no circus was coming. Then he immediately declared August 24 "Sucker Day" in Wetumka. He announced that all refreshments were free! The hot dogs, the soft drinks, the ice cream—all free!

This pleased the people so much that they went into local businesses and spent all the money they had brought for the circus. The town businesspeople watched in amazement as their cash registers filled with money.

"Sucker Day" was so successful, the residents of Wetumka decided to celebrate August 24 every year as Sucker Day. There is a parade and free refreshments. It is the biggest event of the year in little Wetumka.

Several years after F. Morrison's visit, the Wetumka police got a phone call from a sheriff in a small town in Missouri. The sheriff said a man named F. Morrison had just been arrested. Mr. Morrison had sold advertising space in a circus program, but there was no circus. Hadn't he pulled the same trick in Wetumka a few years back? Should the sheriff send F. Morrison to Oklahoma when he finishes his jail sentence in Missouri?

The police chief consulted the businesspeople of Wetumka and then phoned the sheriff in Missouri. No, the people of Wetumka didn't want to bring charges against F. Morrison. F. Morrison, they said, was the best thing that ever happened to Wetumka, Oklahoma.

2. VOCABULARY

LOOKING AT THE STORY

Which words have the same meaning as the words in italics? Write your answer on the line.

arrested	frowned	sentence	the least of their worries
impatient	supplies	consulted	eager
cautious	announced	amazement	attract

1. When the businesspeople of Wetumka heard that a circus was coming to town, they were *very interested*. They were _____ to hear more.

2. The circus would *bring* a lot of people *to* Wetumka. Morrison said it would _____ thousands.

3. Morrison said that businesses should buy all *the things they needed* for crowds of people. "You should get plenty of _____," he said.

4. The businesspeople *didn't smile* when Morrison said that advertising space was very expensive. They all _____.

5. The businesspeople were *very careful* with their money. They were _____ people.

6. The people were *tired of waiting* for the circus. They were getting more _____ by the minute.

7. The money they had lost was *only a small problem* for the business people. Actually, it was _____.

8. After he *declared* August 24 "Sucker Day," the mayor _____ that all refreshments were free.

9. It was *a big surprise* to the business people of Wetumka that they made money on August 24. They watched in _____ as their cash registers filled.

10. A sheriff in Missouri *took Morrison and put him in jail*. After the sheriff _____ Morrison, he called the police chief in Wetumka.

11. Morrison's *punishment* was one year in jail. The sheriff asked, "Should I send him to Oklahoma when he finishes his _____ here?"

12. The police chief *asked* the businesspeople of Wetumka *for their advice*. After he _____ them, he phoned the sheriff in Missouri.

Complete the sentences to show that you understand the meaning of the new words. In small groups, take turns reading your sentences aloud. Ask your classmates questions about their sentences.

1. I would be eager to travel to _____.

2. I am attracted to places that _____.

3. I am cautious when _____.

4. I would frown if I saw _____.

5. I get impatient when _____.

6. If I needed advice, I would consult _____.

3. COMPREHENSION/READING SKILLS

UNDERSTANDING THE MAIN IDEAS

Circle the letter of the best answer.

1. Who was F. Morrison?

　a. He was the publicity man for a circus.

　b. He was the editor of the newspaper in Wetumka, Oklahoma.

　c. He was a man who cheated people out of their money.

2. Why were the businesspeople eager to hear about the circus?

　a. A circus would bring people to Wetumka, and people would spend money in local stores and restaurants.

　b. Most of the businesspeople had children who would enjoy the circus.

　c. Wetumka was very small, so there wasn't much to do; a circus would bring some excitement to the town.

3. Why were the businesspeople willing to pay a lot of money for advertising space in the circus program?

　a. Buying advertising space in the circus program was cheaper than other types of advertising.

　b. They thought that a lot of people would see their advertisements.

　c. Morrison told them that the circus would buy its supplies from the businesses who advertised in the program.

4. How successful was F. Morrison at selling advertising space?

　a. Almost every business in Wetumka bought advertising space.

　b. About half the businesses in Wetumka bought advertising space.

　c. The cautious businesspeople in Wetumka didn't buy advertising space, but Morrison was very successful in Missouri.

5. When the circus didn't come, what was the biggest worry of the businesspeople?

  a. They worried most about the money they had lost.

  b. They worried most about selling all the supplies they had bought.

  c. They worried most about the crowd of hot, impatient people.

6. What did the mayor of Wetumka tell the angry crowd?

  a. He promised them that the circus would be there soon.

  b. He announced that all the refreshments were free.

  c. He told them that Morrison had been arrested in Missouri.

7. How do the people of Wetumka celebrate Sucker's Day every year?

  a. There is a parade and free refreshments.

  b. There is a free circus.

  c. There is music and dancing.

SCANNING FOR INFORMATION

The underlined information is not correct. Find the correct information in the story and write it. Work quickly; try to complete this exercise in three minutes or less.

1. In August <u>1952</u>, a stranger drove into the small town of Wetumka, Oklahoma.

2. He walked into the local <u>real estate</u> office and introduced himself.

3. He said that his name was <u>M</u>. Morrison.

4. Morrison said that a circus would arrive on August <u>23</u>.

5. Morrison said he'd be in town for <u>three</u> weeks, doing publicity for the circus.

6. When Morrison left Wetumka, his <u>briefcase</u> was filled with the money people had paid for advertising space.

7. Thousands of people were waiting along Main Street to watch for the circus, which was to arrive at <u>one o'clock</u>.

8. The <u>police chief</u> of Wetumka declared August 24 Sucker Day.

9. Several years after F. Morrison's visit, the Wetumka police got a call from a sheriff in <u>Kansas</u>.

10. The police chief consulted the businesspeople of Wetumka and then <u>wrote</u> the sheriff that they didn't want to bring charges against Morrison.

4. DISCUSSION

A. Think about these questions. Discuss your answers with your classmates.

Do you know a true story about someone who was cheated out of his or her money? Why do you think people let themselves become suckers? What are some ways to avoid becoming a sucker?

B. Sucker Day is an unusual festival. There are unusual festivals all over the world. For example, there is annual tomato war that takes place in Buñol, Spain. Truckloads of ripe tomatoes are emptied into the main street of the town. Then as many as 20,000 people gather to throw tomatoes at one another! The festival, called "La Tomatina," began in the 1930s, when the town stopped holding bullfights because of their cruelty.

Interview a classmate who has information about an unusual festival. Ask your classmate the questions below. Listen carefully and write your classmate's answers. Then tell the class what you learned.

- What is the name of the festival?
- Where is it?
- When is it?
- What do people do at the festival?
- Do people wear special clothes?
- Do people eat special foods?
- Do you know the history of the festival?
- Have you ever gone to the festival?

5. WRITING

A. Using the information your classmate gave you in the discussion exercise, write a paragraph about an unusual festival. Or write about an unusual festival that you have attended.

B. Write the true story of someone you know who was cheated out of his or her money.

Challenge

F. Morrison told the businesspeople of Wetumka that he had a special opportunity for them. His "business opportunity" was a dishonest trick, and the businesspeople of Wetumka lost all their money.

Below are some other "opportunities." Read the information carefully. Can you guess which of these opportunities are dishonest tricks? (Look in the Answer Key to find out which are dishonest tricks.)

EARN UP TO $2,000 A WEEK
IN YOUR OWN HOME
CHOOSE YOUR OWN HOURS

We are a mail order company, and we need help stuffing our sales brochures into envelopes. Right now, we have so much work on hand that we are paying home workers $2 for each envelope stuffed and returned to us according to our instructions. There is no limit to the number of envelopes that you can stuff for us. Stuff 250 envelopes and get paid $500 . . . Stuff 500 envelopes and get paid $1,000 . . . Stuff 1,000 envelopes and get paid $2,000.

All envelopes will be sent to you with the addresses already typed on and the postage stamps already affixed. That means that you will not have to address any envelopes or buy any postage stamps. Just stuff the envelopes with our brochures and mail them back to us. As soon as we receive your shipment of stuffed envelopes, we'll rush your paycheck to you along with another set of free supplies for stuffing more envelopes.

As a show of good faith, to show us that you are serious about stuffing envelopes for our company, we're going to request that you send us a REFUNDABLE DEPOSIT of $37. The fee will be returned to you as soon as you send us your first 250 stuffed envelopes. At that time we'll send you a check for $537, to cover payment for 250 stuffed envelopes plus a refund of your $37 deposit.

As soon as we have enough home workers, we will withdraw this offer. So please take action today!

MODELS

Earn $100 per hour or $500 per day as a fashion or commercial model. Full or part time. No experience necessary. Real people types, such as children, grandmothers, college students, and construction workers welcome. No fee.

Call now to schedule an interview. If you are selected, we will ask you to provide professional photographs. We will distribute your photos to businesses that are looking for "real-people" models—people like YOU!

③   **$2,000 SCHOLARSHIP GUARANTEED**

Every year millions of dollars in scholarships go unclaimed. You can use this money to finance your college education. Simply pay us a $200 scholarship fee, and we will scan our electronic database and match you with a scholarship. If we can't find at least a $2,000 scholarship for you, we will return your $200.

---

④   **FINAL NOTIFICATION ***** 1999 MODEL CAR**

This is our final notification regarding a 1999 model car we will deliver directly to you. The car is being held in a secured facility awaiting your response. Failure to respond by the posted deadline date will result in forfeiture of the 1999 model car. First, choose the car you would like:

_____ Mustang GT   _____ Honda Accord
_____ Chevy Blazer   _____ Toyota Corolla
_____ Ford Taurus   _____ Dodge Intrepid

Then mail your check for $21.99 to cover the cost of delivery of your car. This is a nationwide offer to promote the sale of selected 1999 1:39 scale model cars. Mail your check for $21.99 today to guarantee delivery of the car of your choice.

---

⑤   **$100,000 IN 60 DAYS!**

Please don't throw this letter away until you have carefully considered what I am about to show you. This could be the most important communication you will ever receive.

FOLLOW THE INSTRUCTIONS BELOW AND IN 20 TO 60 DAYS, YOU WILL RECEIVE $100,000 CASH BY MAIL.

1. **Immediately send $5.00 cash to each of the five names below:**

   - **Fred Hayward, 451 N. Fourth St., Indiana, PA 15701**
   - **Jaime Nelson, 13760 Rose Lane, South Holland, IL 60473**
   - **John Harvey, 7933 Pond Road, Whitewater, WI 53190**
   - **Suzanne Petersen, 13 Lois Lane, Chicago, IL 60643**
   - **Gary Smiles, 230 Fresno Ave., Santa Cruz, CA 95060**

2. **Remove the FIRST name, move the other names up and place your name in the fifth position.**

3. **Print 100 copies of this letter showing your name in the fifth position. Mail the 100 letters. (Do not put your return address on the envelopes.)**

That's all there is to it! Within 20 to 60 days, you will receive $100,000 in cash. The fact that you have received this letter shows that it works!

UNIT **15**

1. PRE-READING

The woman in the picture is running in the city of Sarajevo. What do you know about Sarajevo? Tell the class.

Love Under Siege

On a Sunday afternoon in 1992, Eric Adam sat folding laundry in the living room of his small apartment. He was half-listening to the news on TV and trying not to think back.

Two years ago, Eric had been happy; he was engaged to marry a wonderful woman named Suzi. But Eric's happiness ended suddenly. Suzi, who had a weak heart, died of a heart attack. She was thirty-three years old. Now, two years after Suzi's death, Eric was still struggling with his grief. As he sat on his sofa, folding laundry, his thoughts kept returning to Suzi.

The news on TV was about the summer Olympics. A reporter was talking about a young woman from Bosnia. She was a runner who was training for the Olympics. Twice a day, she ran through the streets of Sarajevo. "Sarajevo?" Eric wondered. There was a war going on in the city of Sarajevo. How could anyone train for the Olympics in Sarajevo? Eric stopped folding laundry and looked at the TV. On the screen, a young woman in a track suit was running through Sarajevo's streets. She was running with her head held high, even though snipers occasionally tried to shoot her. She ran straight toward the camera and then she was gone. The news report was over.

Eric stared at the TV. He was stunned. What courage the woman had! Eric wanted to meet this woman. That wouldn't be easy. She lived halfway around the world, and Eric didn't even know her name.

Eric went to the library and began looking through newspapers. Finally, he found what he was looking for—a photo of the young woman running through the streets of Sarajevo. Under the photo was the woman's name: Mirsada Buric. From the newspapers, Eric learned that Mirsada was no longer in Sarajevo. She was at the summer Olympic games in Barcelona, Spain.

Eric wrote Mirsada a letter. He wrote that he had seen her on TV and wanted her to know that "there is someone in America who admires you. If I can help you in any way, please let me know."

Mirsada's Olympic race was the 3,000 meters. Mirsada didn't win, but when she crossed the finish line, the people in the stadium stood and cheered. They had seen Mirsada on TV, running through the streets of Sarajevo. In the eyes of the crowd, Mirsada was a winner.

After the Olympics, Mirsada couldn't return to Sarajevo because it was too dangerous. She went to Slovenia, a country north of Bosnia, as a refugee. Without her family, Mirsada was lonely.

She thought about Eric's letter and decided to answer it, with the help of her Bosnian-English dictionary. Eric answered her letter and sent a picture of himself. For the next few months, letters flew back and forth between Eric and Mirsada. Finally, Eric wrote that he was flying to Slovenia.

At nine o'clock in the evening, Mirsada stood on a street corner in Slovenia, waiting for Eric. A small car pulled up, and a young man with brown hair and blue eyes stepped out of the car. It was Eric. He ran to Mirsada, smiling. "How are you?" Eric asked. "Fine," Mirsada answered. Then they looked at each other and laughed. Eric couldn't speak Bosnian, and Mirsada couldn't speak English. Eric went to the car and got the woman who was translating for him.

Mirsada, Eric, and the translator went to Mirsada's apartment, where Eric and Mirsada talked until sunrise. Then Eric had to go, or he would miss his flight back to the United States. As he walked toward the car, Eric saw the sadness in Mirsada's eyes. Suddenly he said, "Do you want to come to the United States? There'd be no strings attached—I'll buy a round-trip ticket, so you can go home anytime." Mirsada began to cry. "No," she answered. "Thank you. But no." Eric kissed Mirsada on the cheek and said, "Well, if you ever change your mind, the offer stands." Then he was gone.

Mirsada thought about Eric's offer for weeks. Finally, she decided to go to the United States.

In March 1993, nine months after Eric first saw her on TV, Mirsada arrived in Phoenix, Arizona. She moved into Eric's apartment, where she and Eric lived together like a brother and a sister.

Mirsada studied English. She started college. She ran in dozens of races and won most of them. And, she fell in love with Eric, who was already in love with her. In December, they were married.

In the summer of 1996, the Olympic torch passed through Phoenix, Arizona on its way to the games in Atlanta, Georgia. Mirsada was chosen to carry the torch through Phoenix. As Mirsada ran through the cheering crowd, she thought about everything she had done since the last Olympics. She had come to the United States, learned English, and graduated from college. She had won races. She had fallen in love and gotten married. And now she was carrying the Olympic torch through the streets of Phoenix. She ran as she had run through the streets of Sarajevo—with her head held high.

2. VOCABULARY

LOOKING AT THE STORY

Write the correct word or words on the line.

track suit	no strings attached	refugee	cheered
occasionally	grief	laundry	engaged
stunned	trained	thoughts kept returning	admires

1. Eric washed his clothes. Then he sat on the sofa and folded his

    _____.

2. Eric was going to get married. He was _____ to a woman named Suzi.

3. Eric was fighting his feelings of sadness about Suzi's death. He was still struggling with his _____.

4. Eric couldn't stop thinking about Suzi. His _____ to her.

5. The runner on TV was preparing for the Olympics. She _____ by running through the streets of Sarajevo twice a day.

6. In the picture on page 114, Mirsada is wearing a _____.

7. Sometimes men with guns tried to kill people in Sarajevo. Mirsada ran even though snipers _____ tried to shoot her.

8. Eric was very surprised to see a woman running through he streets of Sarajevo; he couldn't believe it. When the news report was over, he stared at the TV and didn't move. He was _____.

9. After seeing her on TV, Eric had a high opinion of Mirsada. He wrote her, "Someone in the United States _____ you."

10. When Mirsada crossed the finish line, the people in the stadium shouted with happiness. They _____ because they knew how difficult the race was for Mirsada.

11. Mirsada couldn't return to her country because it was too dangerous. So, she went to Slovenia as a _____.

12. Eric told Mirsada he would buy her a round-trip ticket to the United States. He didn't want anything from her in return. He told her that there would be

    _____.

LOOKING AT A NEW CONTEXT

Complete the sentences to show that you understand the meaning of the new words. In small groups, take turns reading your sentences aloud. Ask your classmates questions about their sentences.

1. Something I do only occasionally is _____.

2. Someone whose courage I admire is _____.

3. A sports team I cheer for is _____.

4. An Olympic sport I would love to train for is _____.

5. A person my thoughts keep returning to is _____.

6. A place my thoughts keep returning to is _____.

3. COMPREHENSION/READING SKILLS

UNDERSTANDING CAUSE AND EFFECT

Find the best way to complete each sentence. Write the letter of your answer on the line.

1. Eric was struggling with grief _____

2. Eric couldn't believe a runner was training in Sarajevo _____

3. Eric wanted to meet Mirsada _____

4. For a week, Eric looked through newspapers _____

5. As she ran through the streets of Phoenix, Mirsada held her head high _____

a. because he wanted to know the name of the Bosnian runner he had seen on TV.

b. because there was a war there.

c. because she was proud of everything she had done.

d. because Suzi had died.

e. because he admired her courage.

UNDERSTANDING SUPPORTING DETAILS

Read each sentence on the left. Which sentences on the right give you more information? Match the sentences. Write the letter of your answer on the line.

1. *Eric was happy.* _____

2. The reporter on TV was talking about *a young woman from Bosnia.* _____

3. Eric sent Mirsada *a letter.* _____

4. *Mirsada's race* was the 3,000 meters. _____

5. Mirsada thought about *everything she had done.* _____

a. She was a runner who was training for the Olympics by running through the streets of Sarajevo twice a day.

b. He was engaged to marry a wonderful woman named Suzi.

c. He wrote that he had seen Mirsada on TV and that he admired her.

d. She had come to the United States, learned English, graduated from college, won races, fallen in love, and gotten married.

e. She didn't win, but people cheered when she crossed the finish line.

4. DISCUSSION

Eric and Mirsada's first child was born in 1998. When their daughter is older, they can tell her the amazing story of how they met.

What about your parents? Your grandparents? Your married classmates? How did they meet? Interview someone who is married. First, with the help of your classmates and your teacher, make a list of questions you could ask, such as:

- How old were you when you met?

- Where did you meet?

- What did you think when you saw her/him for the first time?

- _____

- _____

- _____

- _____

- _____

- _____

Ask someone who is married the questions. Listen carefully and write down the answers. Then tell the class what you learned.

5. WRITING

Write the love story of how you or someone you know met his/her spouse. Here is what one student wrote.

When I was 24 years old, I came to the United States from Mexico to live with my aunt. I was her housekeeper. My aunt and her sons treated me very badly. My day started at 5:00 A.M. I had to cook all their meals, clean their shoes, and pick up their clothes. I had to clean the house very well because when my aunt came home, she wiped her hand over the furniture looking for dust. When everybody went to sleep, I began to iron.

In the spring, I ironed in an enclosed porch with lots of windows. Every night a young man stood on the porch next door and watched me iron, but he never spoke to me.

One summer day I went to the store, and he started walking by my side. For the first time he spoke to me. He wondered why they treated me so badly. His house was so close he could hear when they screamed at me. He told me if I wanted to go back to Mexico, he would buy me an airplane ticket, but I did not go. I needed the $10 a week that my aunt paid me and that I sent to my family in Mexico.

That was 29 years ago. I am married to the man who was looking at me on the porch. We celebrated our 28th anniversary. I love him very much. He is a caring man with a big heart and he is a wonderful father and husband. I thank God for him.

Challenge

Robert Fulghum is the author of a book titled *True Love.* The book is a collection of true love stories that ordinary people told him. How did he collect these stories? He sat in coffee houses in Seattle next to a sign that said, "TELL ME A SHORT LOVE STORY AND I WILL BUY YOU COFFEE AND MAKE YOU FAMOUS." The sign always drew a crowd. Once a crowd gathered, Fulghum encouraged people to tell their love stories. He wrote down the best stories and published them in the book. Here are two love stories from Fulghum's book. He says these stories are even better when read aloud to someone you love.

Read the love stories.

Flowers

You wanted really short love stories. This one's long but small. I go to the Pike Place Market in Seattle almost every Saturday morning to shop and carry on a love affair.

For several years I've bought flowers from a youngish woman who is a refugee from one of the hill tribes of Indochina. For one thing, she has the freshest and most beautiful flowers. For another, she is a fresh and beautiful flower herself. I don't know her name, nor she mine. We don't speak the same language. To her, I must be just another customer.

She is spring to me. She's there with pussywillows, daffodils, and then irises. She's summer, with roses and sunflowers. She's fall, with dahlias and chrysanthemums. As the growing season comes to an end, she brings stems of fall leaves to sell, and then it's over. In winter, I miss her.

When we exchange flowers and money, I always try to briefly and slyly touch her hand. I always insist she keep the change and she always insists on giving me an extra flower.

Once I tried to buy all her flowers at once, but she just shook her head. "No." I don't know why. Maybe she, too, is in love with someone and wants to be there to sell him flowers when he comes.

Peanuts

This is really my mother's love story. I asked her to tell you, but she's too shy. It's too good not to pass on. It explains why my brother and I say we owe our existence to peanuts.

When she graduated from high school my mother had everything going for her but one. She was pretty, smart, and came from a well-to-do family, but she was terribly shy, especially around men. Boys didn't like to take her out because she was so quiet. She went off to the same college her mother went to and to please her mother, she agreed to join her mother's sorority. At the first sorority party, she sat out of sight at one end of a room in a corner by a table that had snacks on it. She ate a lot of peanuts out of nervousness.

She began to notice a waiter, who seemed to be as shy as she. He never said anything, but he was taking care of her. He kept her glass filled with nonalcoholic punch and kept her peanut bowl full. From time to time their eyes met and they smiled at each other.

When the dancing started and the party got rowdy, she walked into the kitchen and out the back door to escape. As she was going down the alley, she heard someone calling, "Wait, wait, please wait." It was the waiter, running down the alley after her with a paper bag in his hands. They stood in awkward silence, just smiling. Then he reached into the bag, pulled out a whole can of peanuts and offered them to her and said, "I only wish these were pearls."

He ran back up the alley and into the sorority house.

Well, one thing led to another.

Twenty-five years later, on the silver wedding anniversary of my mother and the waiter (my father), he gave her a sterling silver jar marked "peanuts." She thought that was the gift and was really pleased. But there was more. When she lifted the lid, inside was a string of pearls. No gift ever pleased her more. She wore those pearls as her only jewelry for years. When my father was killed in a traffic accident, she put the silver peanut can in his coffin with him. I've never seen her wear the pearls since. I think I know where they are, but I'm too shy to ask.

Now discuss these questions:

- Robert Fulghum heard hundreds of love stories. Why do you think he chose these two for his book?
- Which story do you like better—"Flowers" or "Peanuts"?

ANSWER KEY

UNIT 1 ———————————————————

Vocabulary
Looking at the Story
1. prize **2.** misbehaves **3.** leather **4.** hose **5.** glued/silverware
6. scissors **7.** sneaked **8.** curtains **9.** Fortunately **10.** rarely
11. kicked

Comprehension/Reading Skills
Understanding the Main Ideas
1. d **2.** b **3.** b **4.** a

Understanding Details
1. ~~Korean~~/French **2.** ~~best~~/worst **3.** ~~200~~/72,000 **4.** ~~good~~/bad
5. ~~boy~~/girl

Challenge
The psychiatrists believe the difference in the way the
questionnaires were completed could have affected the
results of their study in two ways:

1. In Puerto Rico, parents from all over the island completed
   the questionnaire. So, every socio-economic group was
   represented. In Sweden, only parents from an affluent
   suburb completed the questionnaire, so only a high socio-
   economic group was represented. Parents from high socio-
   economic groups usually report fewer problems with their
   children than parents from low socio-economic groups.
2. Only 84 percent of the questionnaires were returned in
   Sweden. Perhaps parents who were having a lot of
   problems with their children did not return the
   questionnaires. (Or some children made sure their
   parents never got the questionnaires in the first place!)

UNIT 2 ———————————————————

Vocabulary
Looking at the Story
1. a **2.** a **3.** a **4.** b **5.** b **6.** a **7.** a **8.** b **9.** b **10.** a **11.** b **12.** a

Comprehension/Reading Skills
Understanding the Main Ideas
1. b **2.** a **3.** b **4.** c **5.** c **6.** b **7.** b

Understanding Supporting Details
1. c **2.** e **3.** a **4.** d **5.** b

Challenge
1. c
In Thailand, it is insulting to point your foot at a person.
2. b
In Korea, it is polite for seated passengers on buses to hold
the packages of those standing. This is usually done without
speaking.

3. b
In France, the customer and the shop owner or salesperson
greet one another when the customer enters the shop and say
good-bye when the customer leaves.
4. c
In Nepal, the cost of many things is based on how much the
customer can afford to pay. Generally, foreigners are richer
than Nepalis, so the shop owner charged you more for the tea
than he charged the Nepali man. To the Nepali, it is fair. So, it
is best to quietly pay the seven rupees.
5. c
Americans are very busy—so busy that some people don't
want to take the time to make friends. To make friends in the
United States, you may have to be assertive and take the first
step.
6. a
"A" is all you need to do. Most utility companies in the United
States are fair. The first people who call get the first available
appointment. (This is called a first-come, first-served basis.)
7. a
In Malaysia, many people are Muslim. Their religion does not
permit them to touch a dog or be touched by a dog. (There
are, however, some Muslims who have dogs.)
8. c
It is probably a good idea to turn down the invitation. If the
family wanted you to stay for dinner, they would have invited
you for dinner.
9. c
The pace of living is slower in Spain than in other countries,
and some people do not worry about being on time. Perhaps
the best solution is to do what Spaniards do: bring knitting, a
book, or a puzzle to pass the time while you wait.
10. c
It is impolite to ask questions about a French person's
personal life. (The question that is a conversation-opener in
the United States—"What do you do for a living?"—is
considered especially impolite in France.) The French would
rather talk about politics, history, or the arts.

UNIT 3 ———————————————————

Vocabulary
Looking at the Story
1. grown **2.** triplets **3.** journey **4.** mules **5.** shack **6.** obvious
7. against **8.** orphanage **9.** adopted **10.** consider

Looking at Special Expressions
1. c **2.** b **3.** a **4.** f **5.** d **6.** e **7.** h **8.** i **9.** g

Comprehension/Reading Skills
Understanding the Main Ideas
1. c **2.** c **3.** c **4.** c **5.** b **6.** c

Scanning for Information
1. 30 **2.** 21 **3.** Argentina **4.** Chile **5.** two **6.** triplets **7.** 20
8. Colina **9.** five **10.** three

UNIT 4

Vocabulary
Looking at the Story
1. a **2.** b **3.** b **4.** a **5.** b **6.** b **7.** a **8.** a **9.** b **10.** a

Looking at Special Expressions
1. c **2.** a **3.** b

Comprehension/Reading Skills
Understanding the Main Ideas
1. c **2.** c **3.** b **4.** a **5.** c **6.** c

Understanding Supporting Details
1. d **2.** c **3.** a **4.** b

Challenge
1. a. N b. P **2.** a. P b. N **3.** a. P b. N

UNIT 5

Vocabulary
Looking at the Story
1. a **2.** a **3.** a **4.** a **5.** a **6.** b **7.** b **8.** b **9.** b **10.** a **11.** a **12.** b

Comprehension/Reading Skills
Understanding Cause and Effect
1. c **2.** d **3.** a **4.** c **5.** b

Understanding Time Relationships
1. 79 **2.** TODAY **3.** 79 **4.** 1860s **5.** 79 **6.** 79 **7.** 1860s **8.** 79 **9.** 79
10. TODAY

Challenge
a. 2 **b.** 1 **c.** 4 **d.** 3 **e.** 5

UNIT 6

Vocabulary
Looking at the Story
1. a **2.** a **3.** b **4.** a **5.** a **6.** a **7.** a **8.** b **9.** b **10.** b **11.** a **12.** b

Looking at Special Expressions
1. b **2.** a **3.** c **4.** d **5.** f **6.** e **7.** i **8.** h **9.** g **10.** k **11.** j **12.** l **13.** m
14. n **15.** o

Comprehension/Reading Skills
Understanding Cause and Effect
1. b **2.** a **3.** d **4.** e **5.** c

Understanding Details
1. dollars/cents **2.** train/bus **3.** Washington/New York **4.** driver/
passenger **5.** foot/shoulder

Challenge
1. a Friday sandwich	a fried-egg sandwich
2. a lonely child	an only child
3. the best diamond rings	the best onion rings
4. hot socks	hot sauce
5. X-rated	x-rayed
6. self of steam	self-esteem
7. for Richard Stans	for which it stands
8. free eye screening	free ice cream
9. euthanasia	youth in Asia
10. ten issues	tennis shoes

UNIT 7

Vocabulary
Looking at the Story
1. a **2.** b **3.** a **4.** b **5.** a **6.** a **7.** a **8.** b **9.** a **10.** a **11.** b **12.** a

Looking at Special Expressions
1. b **2.** a **3.** c **4.** d **5.** f **6.** e **7.** i **8.** g **9.** h **10.** k **11.** j **12.** l

Comprehension/Reading Skills
Understanding Cause and Effect
1. c **2.** e **3.** a **4.** d **5.** b

Understanding Details
1. paint/dust **2.** Rome/Paris **3.** new/old **4.** $30/$3
5. mathematics/geography

Challenge
Christie's sold the items for these amounts:

Andy Warhol painting:	$3.5 million
Lincoln letter:	$442,500
Diana's gown:	$200,000
Steiff teddy bear:	$38,000

UNIT 8

Vocabulary
Looking at the Story
1. b **2.** b **3.** a **4.** a **5.** a **6.** a **7.** a **8.** b **9.** a **10.** b **11.** b **12.** b

Looking at Special Expressions
1. c **2.** a **3.** b **4.** e **5.** f **6.** d **7.** h **8.** i **9.** g

Comprehension/Reading Skills
Understanding the Main Ideas
Children are usually not superstitious. It is always a good idea
to take a numerologist's advice. People who use purple towels
are silly.

Understanding Supporting Details
1. d **2.** e **3.** c **4.** a **5.** b

Challenge
1. b **2.** e **3.** f **4.** c **5.** g **6.** d **7.** a

UNIT 9

Vocabulary
Looking at the Story
1. reminded 2. headed 3. rear bumper 4. came to 5. realistic
6. fool 7. detail 8. essentially 9. spread by word of mouth

Looking at Special Expressions
1. b 2. a 3. c 4. f 5. e 6. d 7. i 8. g 9. h

Comprehension/Reading Skills
Understanding the Main Ideas
Urban legends: are not true; often take place in or near cities;
are realistic; are friend-of-a-friend stories; have many details;
remain essentially the same no matter how far they travel.

Understanding Cause and Effect
1. e 2. d 3. c 4. a 5. b

Challenge
The story about the dog that swallowed the cellular phone (#4)
is true. It was reported in five reputable newspapers: the
Washington Post, the *Boston Herald,* the *Montreal Gazette,* the
Orange County Register, and the London *Daily Telegraph.* So,
the story is (almost certainly) true.

UNIT 10

Vocabulary
Looking at the Story
1. meadow 2. surrounding 3. pirates/treasure 4. shovel
5. chest 6. examining 7. convinced 8. drills 9. investors
10. raised 11. enormous

Looking at Special Expressions
1. b 2. a 3. c

Comprehension/Reading Skills
Understanding Time Relationships
1. c 2. c 3. d 4. b 5. c

Scanning for Information
1. McGinnis 2. oak 3. The next day 4. Two 5. 13 6. Eight
7. evening 8. 1850 9. five 10. 20

UNIT 11

Prereading
the United States; present time

Vocabulary
Looking at the Story
1. a 2. a 3. a 4. b 5. b 6. b 7. b 8. a 9. b 10. b 11. b 12. a

Comprehension/Reading Skills

Understanding the Main Ideas
1. c 2. c 3. a 4. d

Understanding Supporting Details
1. c 2. e 3. a 4. d 5. b

Challenge
a. 2 b. 1 c. 3 d. 5 e. 4

UNIT 12

Vocabulary
Looking at the Story
1. b 2. a 3. a 4. b 5. a 6. a 7. b 8. a 9. a 10. a 11. a 12. b
13. b

Looking at Special Expressions
1. c 2. b 3. a

Comprehension/Reading Skills
Understanding the Main Ideas
1. d 2. b 3. c 4. d 5. c 6. b

Scanning for Information
1. two 2. California 3. 35 4. Passover 5. 24 6. two 7. Thomas
8. Declaration of Independence 9. 1776 10. 50

Challenge
1. b 2. d

UNIT 13

Vocabulary
Looking at the Story
1. elderly 2. demanded 3. unarmed 4. spot 5. accelerator
6. sped 7. ran 8. courtyard 9. hesitated 10. grazed
11. windshield 12. captured

Looking at Special Expressions
1. c 2. a 3. b 4. d 5. f 6. e

Comprehension/Reading Skills
Understanding Time Relationships
1. b 2. d 3. c 4. d 5. d

Understanding Details
1. Spain/France 2. bicycles/car 3. policeman/gunman
4. Barcelona/Paris 5. daughter/wife

UNIT 14

Vocabulary
Looking at the Story
1. eager 2. attract 3. supplies 4. frowned 5. cautious
6. impatient 7. the least of their worries 8. announced
9. amazement 10. arrested 11. sentence 12. consulted

Comprehension/Reading Skills
Understanding the Main Ideas
1. c 2. a 3. c 4. a 5. c 6. b 7. a

Scanning for Information
1. 1950 2. newspaper 3. F. 4. 24 5. two 6. suitcase 7. noon
8. mayor 9. Missouri 10. phoned

Challenge
All five "opportunities" are dishonest tricks. This is how each
trick works:

1. When people send in their $37 deposit, they do not get
   envelopes and sales brochures. They might get instructions
   on how to place ads like the one they responded to, so that
   they can cheat other people out of their money. (So, they

will be stuffing envelopes, but not for a legitimate business.) Or they might get a list of companies that are supposedly interested in having people stuff envelopes.

2. This is probably a trick. The models who are "selected" by the modeling agency will be asked to sign a contract agreeing to pay several hundred dollars for professional photographs. Sometimes the modeling agency never distributes the photos to businesses, and sometimes the agency never even gives the potential models their photos. The company simply packs up and leaves town.

3. This ad guarantees that "we will match you with a scholarship." That only means they will give you *information* about a possible scholarship; it doesn't mean that you will actually get the scholarship. Scholarship information is available free from most U.S. universities and high schools.

4. What is a "1999 model car"? It could be two things: (1.) a car that was built in 1999 (a 1999 model), or, (2.) a model car—that is, a small reproduction of a car built in 1999. This offer is for a 1999 1:39 scale model car. That means that for your $21.99 you will get a model car that is one-thirty-ninth the size of a real car. (And they are keeping these little cars, probably made of plastic, in a "secured facility"!)

5. This is a classic chain letter. The idea that everyone who participates in a chain letter will make money is mathematically impossible. This particular chain letter asks you to send the letter on to 100 people. Each of those 100 people would then send the letter on to 100 more people. Each of those 10,000 people would send the letter on to 100 more people. If everyone who received a letter sent it on to 100 people, by the fifth mailing, ten billion people would receive the letter. That's more than the population of the world! The very first investors in the chain might receive money, but later investors rarely get back their original investments ($25 for the five people on the list, plus the cost of copying and mailing the letter). Also, this type of chain letter is illegal in the United States.

UNIT 15

Vocabulary
Looking at the Story
1. laundry 2. engaged 3. grief 4. thoughts kept returning
5. trained 6. track suit 7. occasionally 8. stunned 9. admires
10. cheered 11. refugee 12. no strings attached

Comprehension/Reading Skills
Understanding Cause and Effect
1. d 2. b 3. e 4. a 5. c

Understanding Supporting Details
1. b 2. a 3. c 4. e 5. d

CREDITS

We wish to acknowledge the following sources of information and ideas:

(for page 8) The information in the graph is from "Comparisons of Problems Reported by Parents in 12 Cultures" in the *Journal of the American Academy of Child and Adolescent Psychiatry,* September 1997.

(for page 9) The questionnaire is adapted from the "Child Behavior Checklist" developed by psychiatrist Thomas Achenbach.

(for page 15) Discussion Exercise 4A is the idea of Jean Stocker, TESL-L on-line discussion group, 7 April 1999.

(for pages 16–17) The quiz on cultures and customs is from:

Culture Shock! France by Sally Taylor. Singapore: Times Books International, 1995.
Culture Shock! Italy by Raymond Flower and Alessandro Falassi. Singapore: Times Books International, 1995.
Culture Shock! Korea by Sonja Vegdahl Hur and Ben Seunghwa Hur. Singapore: Times Books International, 1988.
Culture Shock! Malaysia by Heidi Nunan. Singapore: Times Books International, 1991.
Culture Shock! Nepal by Jon Burbank. Singapore: Times Books International, 1994.
Culture Shock! Spain by Marie Louise Graffe. Singapore: Times Books International, 1993.
Culture Shock! Thailand by Robert and Nanthapa Cooper. Singapore: Times Books International, 1982.

(for page 23) Discussion Exercise 4B ("Invisible Pictures") is from *The Recipe Book* by Seth Lindstromberg, Longman, 1990.

(for page 24) "Full House" was adapted from "Full House" by Dennis Covington, *Redbook,* December 1993.

(for pages 48–49) The misunderstandings were compiled from:

- The "Kids Have a Way with Words" column in *Taste of Home* magazine, P.O. Box 992, Greendale, WI 53129 (#1 and #4);
- the web site of Medical Transcriptionists Daily (#5);
- Mrs. Nielsen's Student Bloopers page, Mount Logan (Utah) Middle School's web site (#6);
- The "Life in these United States" feature of *Reader's Digest* magazine (#3 May 1999, p. 76 and #8 Jan. 1999, p. 80);
- *More Anguished English* by Richard Lederer, Delacorte Press, 1993 (#10).

(for page 51) "A Real Bargain" is adapted from "Paris Map May Show Man Route to Riches," by Jo Ellen Meyers Sharp, the *Indianapolis Star,* 17 August 1985.

(for page 67) The urban legends are from the following books by Jan Harold Brunvand:

The Vanishing Hitchhiker: American Urban Legends and Their Meanings. Norton, 1981.
The Choking Doberman and Other "New" Urban Legends. Norton, 1984.
The Mexican Pet: More "New" Urban Legends and Some Old Favorites. Norton, 1986.
Curses! Broiled Again! The Hottest Urban Legends Going. Norton, 1989.
The Baby Train: And Other Lusty Urban Legends. Norton, 1993.

(for page 75) "The Secret of Oak Island," adaptation by permission of the National Geographic Society, copyright © June 1989, *World* magazine.

(for page 91) The statistics on the death rates of elderly Chinese women and elderly Jewish men are the findings of David Phillips as reported in *Lancet* (1988) and the *Journal of the American Medical Association* (1990).

(for page 96) The "cutting the lemon" guided imagery is from the web site of the Academy for Guided Imagery in Mill Valley, CA. It was written by the academy's co-director, Dr. Martin L. Rossman.

(for page 97) The guided imagery scripts are from *Staying Well with Guided Imagery* by Belleruth Naparstek, Warner Books, 1994.

(for page 99) "An Unexpected Adventure" is adapted from "A Lille, vraie-fausse prise d'otage dans la cour de la gendarmerie," *La Voix du Nord,* 8 August 1989.

(for page 105) "A Wild Ride" is reprinted with permission of the Associated Press.

(for pages 112–113) The "dishonest tricks" are actual scams that people in the United States received in the mail. They were provided by the U.S. Postal Inspection Service. Information about the way the scams work was provided by the Wisconsin Department of Agriculture, Trade, and Consumer Protection.

(for page 115) To read more about Mirsada Buric, see "Love Under Siege" by Lawrence Elliott in *Reader's Digest,* March 1997.

(for pages 120–121) "Flowers" and "Peanuts" are reprinted from *True Love; Stories Told to and by Robert Fulghum,* HarperCollins Publishers, 1997.

The sentence completion vocabulary activity is the idea of Sally Winn ("Vocabulary Revitalized" by Sally Winn, *TESOL Journal,* Summer 1996).

The format for many of the discussion exercises was inspired by Irene Schoenberg's *Talk About Values, Conversation Skills for Intermediate Students,* Longman, 1989.